PRESENTING
THE QUR'ĀN

Presented to: Joey / Umar

From: Fezal

Date: 03/ /05

QURANIC WISDOM FOR MODERN LIVING

PRESENTING THE QUR'ĀN

A BRIEF INTRODUCTION TO ALL THE 114 CHAPTERS OF THE QUR'ĀN

◆ ◆ ◆

SANIYASNAIN KHAN

Goodword
B·O·O·K·S

To my father, Maulana Wahiduddin Khan

The publisher would like to thank the following persons who made this book possible: Anna Khanna, Farida Khanam, Ruqaiyyah Waris Maqsood, Abdal Hakim Winter, Anis Luqman Nadvi

The text in this book is gleaned from
The Encyclopaedia of the Qur'an

First published 1997
Reprinted 1997, 1998, 2000, 2003

Goodword Books Pvt. Ltd.
1, Nizamuddin West Market
New Delhi 110 013
e-mail: info@goodwordbooks.com
Printed in India

---

www.goodwordbooks.com

CONTENTS

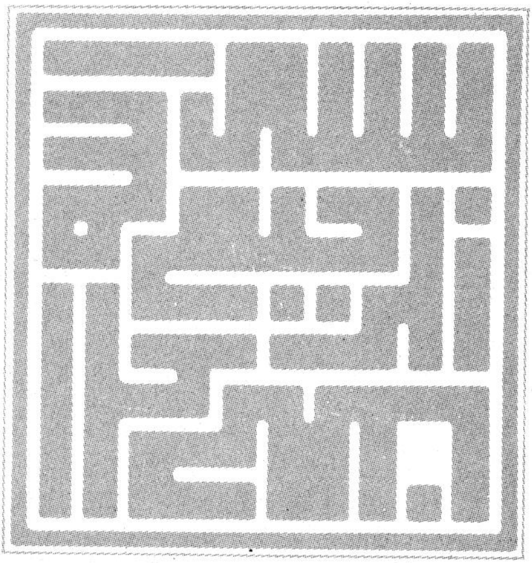

INTRODUCTION

The Qur'ān, which comprises 114 *sūrahs* or chapters, began to be revealed to the Prophet Muḥammad ﷺ, upon whom be peace, through the angel Jibrīl (Gabriel) in A.D. 610, while the Prophet was sitting in seclusion in the cave of Hira, near Makkah. The entire revelation was completed over a period of 23 years, and the last passage of the Qur'ān was revealed to the Prophet while he was addressing a gathering at Mount ʿArafāt after performing his last Ḥajj in A.D. 632. Being the true word of Allah in human language, the Qur'ān is the *eternal book of instruction* for the whole of mankind. It provides correct and understandable answers to all the questions which arise in an inquisitive mind, such as why Allah has placed humanity on earth? What is His scheme of things in creating such a vast universe? How should we lead our lives? What will happen to us after death? And so on.

The Qur'ān is the sacred scripture of Islam. No other scripture, in the history of the human race has ever had such an impact on the lives and hearts of its readers, especially those who first heard its message and then passed it on to later generations.

It presents the key to successful human existence, both in this life and in the life to come. If Allah really exists, and if He is perfect Justice and Compassion, it is a necessary part of His guardianship of humanity to show us which things are pleasing, and which will bring us to success. Conversely, we need to know what things to avoid in order to avert disaster and suffering. These things are all revealed in the Qur'ān.

If Muslims follow the way of life laid down in the Qur'ān, and in the *sunnah* of the Prophet Muḥammad ﷺ, they will understand how to serve Allah and respect the ideal of justice. They will also be imbued with confidence and contentment, and will live in peace. No one is obliged to read the Qur'ān, or forced to believe in it. It is laid in front of an inquirer, with the invitation to use his or her reason to examine what is said, and judge whether its teachings are right or wrong.

Those who live wrongly, in selfishness, arrogance, cruelty and so on, are given a dire warning. They may think that they have safely found success, but that is not the case. This life is not all that there is, and on the Day of Judgement they will be called to account for all that they have done, and avoided doing.

The Qur'ān warns of this inevitability, and urges us to repent and seek forgiveness, and put our lives and hearts on the right lines while there is still time.

This book is a humble attempt to convey the essence of the Qur'ān by presenting the contents of each of its *sūrahs* in condensed form. The focus throughout the book is on the spirit of the Qur'ān, on its message and its teachings and on the lessons that should be derived from it for our daily life. Although the book is primarily intended for the general reader who is interested in studying the Qur'ān, it will also be found a useful tool for *daʿwah*.

In addition to its being the duty of every Muslim man, woman and child to study the Qur'ān and follow it, the communication of its message to non-Muslims is also obligatory. It is pre-eminently the responsibility of the Muslims to convey the Message of the Qur'ān to other nations (5:67; 12:108; 72:28). Therefore, the Qur'ān urges them over and over again to carry out this task and even calls it the true *jihād*: 'By means of this (Qur'ān), strive with them, with the utmost strenuousness' (25:52). In his last sermon the Prophet Muḥammad also urged his followers to convey the message of the Qur'ān 'even if only a single *āyah*.' Therefore, the greatest need of the hour is to acquaint non-Muslims with this message in a language and style which is understandable to them, as the Prophet—and through him all the believers—is enjoined in the Qur'ān: 'O Messenger, proclaim all that is revealed to you from your Lord. Unless you do it fully, you have not conveyed His message (at all). Allah will protect you from all people' (5:67). Thus we must perform this task in all sincerity till the Last Day; therein lies our entire success both in this world and in the world to come.

In the name of Allah,
the Compassionate, the Merciful
Praise be to Allah,
Lord of the Universe,
the Compassionate, the Merciful,
Master of the Day of Judgement.
You alone we worship,
and to You alone we turn for help.
Guide us to the straight path.
The path of those whom You have favoured,
not of those who have incurred Your wrath,
nor of those who are gone astray.

(*Al-Fātiḥah* 1-7)

I

AL-FĀTIHAH

The Opening

It befits us to commence all tasks in the name of Allah, our Master, the source of all mercy and all compassion, whose blessings are continually descending upon creation. To commence any undertaking in His name is to pray that the Almighty, in His infinite mercy, may come to our assistance and bring our work to a successful conclusion. This is our acknowledgement that we are Allah's servants, and it also brings a divine assurance of success.

The Qur'ān has a special way of expressing a believer's inner sentiments in the best possible words. The opening chapter of the Qur'ān constitutes a supplication of this nature, and expresses feelings which are naturally aroused in us after discovering the truth.

When we look at the world around us, we cannot fail to notice Allah's power and mercy in evidence everywhere. With what care Allah watches over the world! Everything has been made to relate to our needs. This observation shows us that the great cosmic machine cannot be in vain. We realize that there must come a day when the ungrateful will be taken to task and the grateful rewarded. We spontaneously entreat our Lord: 'Lord, You are the Master of the Day of

Judgement. I have submitted to You and humbly seek Your help; have mercy on me. Lord, show me the path that is, to You, the true path. Enable me to tread the path of Your chosen servants. Help me to avoid the path of those who have gone astray, and the path of those who have incurred Your wrath due to their obstinacy.'

Allah requires His servants to live their lives with such thoughts and emotions. The opening chapter of the Qur'ān is a miniature picture of such a believer, while the rest of the Qur'ān is an enlargement of it.

2

AL-BAQARAH

The Heifer

This was the first *sūrah* to be revealed at Madīnah, except verses 275-281, which relate to the last months before the Prophet's death. It contains 286 *āyāt*, which makes it the longest *sūrah* of the Qur'ān. The title is derived from the story narrated in *āyāt* 67-73.

The *sūrah* begins by underlining the basic purpose of the revelations of the Qur'ān—namely, the guidance of humanity in spiritual and worldly affairs. The main stress is laid on the contrasting attitudes of those who accept these revelations and those who reject them. Dealing with the fate of disbelievers and hypocrites, the inimitability of the Qur'ān, the story of the Prophet Ādam عليه السلام and the creation of humanity, the *sūrah* goes on to describe in great detail the story of the Banū Isrā'īl and the sins committed by them. Particular attention is drawn to the Prophet Ibrāhīm عليه السلام with his realisation of the oneness of Allah and his building of the Kaʿbah as the direction of prayer for all 'those who surrender themselves to Allah.'

The *sūrah* then sums up the basic teachings and rules of Islam on the subjects of fasting, pilgrimage, charity, usury, food, retaliation, wills, marriage, family affairs, etc., and concludes with a prayer:

Our Lord,
take us not to task
if we forget, or make a mistake.
Our Lord,
charge us not with a load such
as You laid upon those before us.
Our Lord,
do not burden us
beyond what we have the strength to bear.
And pardon us,
and forgive us,
and have mercy on us;
You are our Protector.
And help us against the people
that are unbelievers.

(2:286)

3

ĀL ʿIMRĀN

The House of ʿImrān

The *sūrah* was revealed at Madīnah and contains 200 *āyāt*. It derives its title from *āyah* 33, which refers to the family of ʿImrān, the father of the Prophet Mūsā عليه السلام. The *sūrah* begins by praising Allah, 'who shapes your bodies in your mothers' wombs as He pleases.' *Āyāt* 8 and 9 are a prayer: 'Lord, do not cause our hearts to go astray after you have guided us.' The present life has been made so attractive that people are freely tempted by sexual lust and offspring, hoarded treasures, splendid horses, cattle and plantations. But the life hereafter is surely better than this (3:14). The believers pray, 'Lord we believe in You; forgive our sins and keep us from the torment of the Fire.' They are steadfast, sincere, obedient and charitable, imploring forgiveness at dawn (3:16-17). The *sūrah* goes on to describe how heedless people are of the truth, and says that it is only the Lord who bestows sovereignty on whom He wills, and who takes it away from whom He pleases.

The *sūrah* asserts that 'the day will surely come when each soul will be confronted with whatever good it has done.' Mention is also made of several prophets including Ādam, Nūḥ, Ibrāhīm, Zakariyyā and ʿĪsā, upon all of whom be peace. Maryam (Mary) is cited as one who is exalted above all womankind (3:42). *Āyah* 64 is a key passage of the Qur'ān which calls the People of the Book (Jews and Christians) to the Oneness of God.

The unbelievers who are seeking a religion other than Allah's should know that every single soul in the heavens or on the earth has submitted to Him, willingly or by compulsion (3:83). From those who die unbelievers, no ransom shall be accepted even if it were as much gold as would fill the entire earth (3:91).

The *sūrah* goes on to urge the believers 'to call for righteousness, enjoin justice and forbid evil' (3:104). The Prophet's Companions are called 'the best nation' (3:110) and patience and piety are held up as virtues which will safeguard one against evil conspiracies (3:120). Referring to the calamitous defeat at Uḥud, the *sūrah* says that Allah 'alternates these vicissitudes among people so that He may test them' (3:140). Those who are niggardly in the cause of Allah will be fettered with their own wealth on the Day of Judgement (3:180). Every soul will taste death and the truly triumphant will be those who are spared the Fire and permitted to enter Paradise (3:185). After saying in admonition to believers: 'You shall be tested through your wealth and your persons,' the *sūrah* concludes with the following awe-inspiring prayer:

In the creation of the heavens and earth, and in the alternation of night and day, there are signs for those of sense; those that remember Allah when standing, sitting, and lying down, and reflect on the creation of the heavens and the earth, saying: 'Lord, You have not created this in vain. Glory be to You! Save us from the torment of the Fire.

'Lord, those whom You will cast into the Fire You will put to eternal shame: none will help the evil-doers. Lord, we have heard someone calling to the true faith, saying: "Believe in your Lord," and we believed. Lord, forgive us our sins and remove from us our evil deeds and make us die with the righteous. Lord, grant us what You promised through Your prophets, and do not hold us up to shame on the Day of Resurrection. You will never break Your promise.'

(3:190-193)

4

AN-NISĀ'

The Women

The *sūrah* was revealed at Madīnah and contains 176 *āyāt*. Stressing the essential unity of mankind, the *sūrah* begins with an appeal for the solidarity of the human race, and makes special mention of the rights of orphans. A large portion of the *sūrah,* as its title indicates, deals with the rights of women and the many-faceted questions relating to family life, such as the law of inheritance, marital relations and the prohibition of marriage with close relations.

Āyāt 7 to 23 mainly deal with family affairs, social teachings, orphans, business transactions, and so on. Male believers are asked to treat their wives with kindness, even if they dislike them, because 'it may be that you dislike a thing which Allah has meant for your own abundant good' (4:19). Those who desire 'to exchange one wife for another' should not take away anything from the *qinṭār* (treasure) which they have given them. The allusion to the 'exchange' of one wife for another clearly indicates that the Qur'ān desires stable marriages (4:20). In matters of marital disputes (and in wider terms, of every dispute), the *sūrah* says 'reconciliation is best' (4:127) and elsewhere also points out the method of arbitration in such cases.

The *sūrah* categorically states that Allah may

forgive everything except that 'partners should be set up with Him' (4:48, 116). *Āyah* 78 says that any good or evil that befalls one comes only from Allah. Believers are instructed to respond to greetings in 'a better way' (4:86). The *sūrah* gives permission to fight (*qitāl*) against those who persecute others (4:75) and goes on to say that if the rival group offers to make peace, they should not be harmed (4:90).

Other subjects that the *sūrah* deals with include the behaviour of the community in war and peace, manslaughter, how to deal with hypocrites, justice, People of the Book, Banū Isrā'īl, rights of parents, stories of the prophets, the importance of prayer, and other topics.

5

AL-MĀ'IDAH

The Table

The *sūrah* belongs to the Madīnan period and contains 120 *āyāt*. It takes its title from the request made by the disciples of the Prophet ʿĪsā عليه السلام that he should pray to his Lord to send down a table spread with food from Heaven (5:112). The *sūrah* deals with Jews and Christians, and with certain details relating to Ḥajj, foods, prayer and social relations, etc. Referring to the murder of the Prophet Ādam's son Hābīl (Abel) by his brother Qābīl (Cain), the *sūrah* declares that 'whoever killed a human being...it shall be as though he had slain all mankind, whereas, if anyone saved a life, it shall be regarded as though he had saved all mankind' (5:32). Referring to the Prophet ʿĪsā عليه السلام, the *sūrah* says that on the Day of Judgement Allah will ask him whether he had ever told people to worship him and his mother as gods besides Allah. But ʿĪsā عليه السلام would disclaim this and say that he had only told them to 'worship Allah, my Lord and your Lord' (5:116-117). The *sūrah* also contains the very last portion of the Qur'ān (5:3), which was revealed to the Prophet during his last pilgrimage while he was addressing the gathering at ʿArafāt.

6

AL-ANᶜĀM

The Cattle

The *sūrah*, revealed at Makkah, contains 165 *āyāt*. Its title derives from references in *āyāt* 136-138 to pre-Islamic practices concerning animals.

Praising Allah, 'Who created the heavens and the earth,' the *sūrah* is censorious of unbelievers who would have disbelieved divine revelations, even if 'a Book inscribed on real parchment' had been sent down to them from heaven (6:7). 'Allah, to punish them, turns away their hearts and their eyes from truth' (6:110). Then, on the Day of Judgement, 'when they are set before the Fire, they will cry out: "Would that we could return! Then we would not deny the revelations of our Lord and would be true believers"' (6:27). Subsequently, it is revealed that 'if Allah wills to guide someone, He opens his (or her) heart to Islam' (6:126).

Āyah 108 instructs believers not to revile the idols of unbelievers, as they too in their ignorance would revile Allah with rancour. The *sūrah* principally concerns Divine attributes and mentions several prophets, including the Prophet Ibrāhīm in his quest for Truth. Near the end is the prayer: 'My prayers and my devotions, my life and my death, are all for Allah, Lord of the Universe' (6:162).

7

AL-AʿRĀF

The Heights

The *sūrah*, revealed at Makkah, contains 206 *āyāt*. The title derives from *āyah* 46, which refers to the Heights, or a raised platform, on which the righteous will gather before entering Paradise.

It begins by mentioning that the Qur'ān is an admonition and warning, then tells the story of the Prophet Ādam عليه السلام and Satan (Iblīs). According to 7:26, the finest clothing is 'the robe of piety.' Depicting scenes of hell, the *sūrah* describes the utter helplessness of sinners who would give anything to live their lives again on earth, so that they might act differently (7:53). 7:56 reminds believers to pray to their Lord with humility and in secret. Then come the stories of the Prophets Nūḥ, Hūd, Ṣāliḥ, Lūṭ, Shuʿayb, Mūsā and Hārūn, upon all of whom be peace.

It also outlines the divine scheme of putting people on trial through hardship and ease: hardship cleanses the believer of sin (7:168).

Recalling the creation of human beings from one soul, the *sūrah* refers to those who pray to Allah for offspring; when Allah gives them a healthy child, they begin to associate others with Allah (7:189). Lamenting this lapse, the Qur'ān says: 'Exalted be Allah above their idols!' (7:190). Finally believers are asked to show forgiveness, speak for justice and avoid the ignorant (7:199) and to remember the Lord humbly, with awe, morning and evening, without raising their voices (7:205).

8

AL-ANFĀL

The Spoils

The *sūrah* was revealed at Madīnah and contains 75 *āyāt*. Its title is taken from the *āyah* which refers to the spoils of the battle of Badr.

The *sūrah* begins by asking the believers to have fear of Allah and end the dispute (regarding the spoils of Badr). 'The true believers are those' according to *āyah* 2, 'whose hearts are filled with awe at the mention of Allah, and when His revelations are recited to them, it increases them in faith, and in their Lord they put their trust.'

The *sūrah* goes on to deal with the battle of Badr and the lessons to be derived from it, and stresses that 'victory comes only from Allah' (8:10). It also exhorts the believers to obey Allah and His Messenger. As a military strategy, the *sūrah* notes that fighting forces should be kept ready so that enemy may be terrified, (8:60) and emphasizes the importance of peace: 'If they incline to peace, you incline to it too' (8:61).

9

AT-TAWBAH

Repentance

This *sūrah,* revealed at Madīnah, contains 129 *āyāt.* Beginning without the *basmala* invocation, it derives its title from *āyah* 104, which refers to Allah accepting repentance from His servants. Also called *Barā'ah*, or 'The Immunity,' its first words are a declaration of immunity from Allah and His Messenger to idolators with whom believers had made agreements. It is later made clear that believers may, however, wage war on those who break these agreements.

The *sūrah* deals mainly with injunctions on situations of war and peace. Believers are allowed to defend themselves against those who attack them first (9:13). It urges them 'to fight against those who have broken their oaths and conspired to banish the Messenger' (9:13) and makes the prophecy that the message of Islam is bound to prevail, though the unbelievers 'want to extinguish the light of Allah with their mouths' (9:32). The *sūrah* also mentions the incident of the Hijrah of the Prophet with Abū Bakr, and their conversation in the cave, when the enemy seemed about to capture them.

The specific objectives of *zakāt* and charity are described in *āyāt* 58-60. Elsewhere, charity is also referred to as a means of cleansing and purifying the believers, and the Prophet Muḥammad ﷺ is asked to pray for people who give generously (9:103). Hypocrites and other non-believing tribes are condemned to suffering, and the Prophet is told that, even if he prayed seventy times to intercede for such people, his prayer would not be answered (9:80). It is pointed out that if the hypocrites knew how close they were to hellfire, they would laugh less and weep more (9:82).

The Muhājirūn and Anṣār—those who migrated and those who helped and supported the migrants—are thus commended: 'Allah is pleased with them and they are pleased with Him' (9:100). It is also stressed that Allah turned in mercy even to those who had not stood by the Prophet in the hour of adversity (9:117).

Āyah 111 states that Allah purchased from the faithful their lives and worldly goods in return for Paradise, and that they should therefore strive with their persons and possessions to spread the message of Islam. They are the ones who repent, who serve Him and praise Him, who fast and who kneel and prostrate themselves, who enjoin justice, forbid evil and observe the commandments of Allah (9:112).

The *sūrah* concludes with a moving passage about the Prophet Muḥammad ﷺ: 'There has now come to you a messenger of your own, one who grieves at your sinfulness and cares for you; one who is benevolent and merciful to true believers.'

10

YŪNUS

Jonah

The *sūrah* belongs to the late Makkan period and contains 109 *āyāt*. It derives its name from the reference to the Prophet Yūnus (Jonah) in *āyah* 98. The chief feature of this *sūrah* is the invocation of the wonderful creations of Allah which are 'signs for righteous people.' *Āyah* 12 reminds us that 'when affliction befalls someone, he (or she) cries out to Us (Allah), lying on his side, sitting, or standing on his feet. But as soon as We relieve his affliction, he pursues his former way, as though he had never prayed for Our help.' The *sūrah* also contains stories of the Prophets Nūḥ عليه السلام and Mūsā عليه السلام.

11

HŪD

The *sūrah* was revealed at Makkah and contains 123 *āyāt*. The *sūrah* derives its title from the reference to the Prophet Hūd عليه السلام (*āyāt* 50-60) who was sent to the ʿĀd people. Disaster overtook them when they failed to respond to his call.

The story of the Prophet Nūḥ (Noah) عليه السلام is dealt with in detail—people's rejection of his call; the making of the Ark; the drowning of his son and finally the settling of the Ark on Mount Jūdī along with the righteous people. Stories of the Prophets Lūṭ, Ṣāliḥ, Shuʿayb and Mūsā, upon all of whom be peace, are also recounted. *Āyah* 6 tells us that 'there is not a creature on this earth but that Allah provides its sustenance. He knows its dwelling and its resting place.' The faithful are also enjoined to 'attend to your prayers morning and evening, and in the night time too. Good deeds shall make amends for sins' (11:114).

12

YŪSUF

Joseph

The *sūrah* was revealed at Makkah and contains 111 *āyāt*. It derives its title from the Prophet Yūsuf's 'most beautiful story,' which takes up almost the entire chapter. Yūsuf was the son of the Prophet Yaʿqūb (Jacob) عليه السلام and himself a great prophet and a 'pious ancestor.'

From a very early age Yūsuf was so brilliant a child that his father loved him more than any of his sons. His half brothers, who were jealous of him, one day threw him into a waterless well. He was later picked up by a caravan, who sold him to ʿAzīz, one of the nobles of Egypt. ʿAzīz's wife made advances to Yūsuf, but he resisted and tried to escape, and his innocence was proved by the fact that his shirt was torn from the back. Despite this proof, he was sent to prison. After some years, having successfully interpreted a dream which had caused the King great concern, he was set free and ultimately made one of the King's ministers. His half brothers came to him, asking for food during a great famine. His father back home was so sad at the loss of Yūsuf that he virtually became blind, but when Yūsuf sent his shirt to his father, his eyesight was restored.

Yūsuf invited his family to Egypt and embraced

them saying: Welcome to Egypt, in safety, if Allah wills! (*udkhulū Miṣra inshā Allāhu āminīn*)! He held his parents in honour and made them sit on the throne. At this time all, including his brothers, bowed to him in respect.

As well as demonstrating the unshakeable faith and highest degree of piety and righteousness of the Prophet Yūsuf, his 'most beautiful story' offers several extraordinary lessons for the faithful. The gentle patience—*ṣabr jamīl*—shown by both the Prophets Yaʿqūb and Yūsuf at the most difficult moments is exemplary; the Prophet Yaʿqūb عليه السلام, having lost both of his beloved sons, merely turned to his Lord saying: 'I complain to Allah of my sorrow and my sadness' (*innamā ashkū baththī wa ḥuznī ila'l Lāh*) (12:86).

13

AR-RAʿD

Thunder

The *sūrah*, revealed at Makkah, with 43 *āyāt* derives its title from *āyah* 13, which testifies to Allah's might with: 'The thunder sounds His praises and the angels, too, for awe of Him.' Rich in content, the *sūrah* describes the creations of Allah as His signs for people of understanding. It gives two important maxims for the individual and the community. One is that 'Allah does not change a people's condition unless they change their own (13:11) i.e. He deprives people of His blessings only when their inner selves become depraved and withholds His blessings from wilful sinners until they change their inner selves.

The other is expressed as a parable: 'He sends down water from the sky, which fills the riverbeds to overflowing, so that the torrent bears a swelling foam, akin to that which rises from smelted ore when men make ornaments and tools. Thus Allah depicts truth and falsehood. The scum is cast away, but that which is of use to man remains behind' (13:17). We are thus urged to be truthful and useful to others lest we be cast away like 'scum.' *Āyah* 14 cites the man who bids water rise to his mouth. But to no avail. This shows that prayer to anyone or anything other than the Lord will surely be in vain.

14

IBRĀHĪM

Abraham

The *sūrah* was revealed at Makkah and contains 52 *āyāt*. It bears the name of the Prophet Ibrāhīm because of the considerable mention it makes of him.

The Prophet Ibrāhīm's prayer in *āyāt* 36-41 for the city of Makkah and for his descendants forms the main theme of the *sūrah*: 'Lord, make this city a land of safety. Preserve me and my descendants from serving idols.'

The *sūrah* says that every prophet spoke to his people in their own language (14:4). It also states that those who thank their Lord for His blessings will have abundance bestowed upon them, but that a terrible punishment awaits the thankless (14:7). It goes on to compare a good word with a good tree, whose roots are firm and whose branches are in the sky, while an evil word is compared with an evil tree, torn out of the earth and shorn of all its roots (14:24-25). It then warns wrongdoers of the Day when they will plead with the Lord to grant them respite so that they may respond to His call. But it will be too late. They will be reminded that they used to swear that no kind of resurrection or retribution awaited them. 'On that Day when the earth will be changed into a different earth and the heavens into new heavens, mankind shall stand before Allah, the One, who holds absolute sway over all that exists.' And 'Allah will reward each soul according to its deeds' (14:51). The *sūrah* ends with the call to worship Allah: 'This is a warning to mankind. Let them take heed and know that He is but one God. Let the wise bear this in mind' (14:52).

15

AL-ḤIJR

The Rocky Tract

The *sūrah*, which is named after a rocky tract of that name about 150 miles north of Madīnah, was revealed at Makkah and contains 99 *āyāt*. Its main theme is the lesson to be drawn from the stories of how the people of al-Ḥijr and al-Aykah were destroyed when they rejected the call of the prophets. The people of the Prophet Lūṭ عليه السلام were also destroyed for their unspeakable crimes. The *sūrah* sets forth the important cosmic principle that Allah had never destroyed any people 'whose term of life was not ordained beforehand' (15:4). In *āyah* 9, Allah declares: 'It was We that revealed the Qur'ān, and it is We who shall guard it (from all corruption).' This prophecy has been proved true by the striking fact that the Qur'ān has remained free of even the slightest interpolation for a period of over 1400 years. The *sūrah* concludes by enjoining the Prophet in particular and the believers in general to worship their Lord till they die (15:99).

16

AN-NAḤL

The Bee

The *sūrah* was revealed at Makkah and contains 128 *āyāt*. The title of the *sūrah* is derived from *āyah* 68, which refers to Allah's command to the bees 'to make their lives on the mountains, in the trees and on the buildings, to feed on every kind of fruit and to follow the path of the Lord.' Later on honey is called a 'healing for humanity.' The *sūrah* stresses the blessings and wonders of the Almighty and reminds us of the bounties that Allah has showered on mankind. *Āyah* 58 deplores the hostile attitude of some men towards the female child: 'When news of a newborn girl is announced to him, his face darkens, and he is filled with suppressed anger.' In cows there is a great lesson too. They give us pure milk to drink, coming out of their bellies 'between the bowels and the blood' (16:66). In *āyah* 90 Allah enjoins justice, kindness and charity to one's kindred, and forbids indecency, wickedness and oppression. Due to its comprehensive moral teachings, this *āyah* was ordered by the Caliph ʿUmar ibn al-Khaṭṭāb to be regularly recited in every sermon of the Friday prayer, and since that time this has been the regular practice. Enjoining us to fulfil our promises, the *sūrah* warns us not to be like a 'woman who unravels the threads she has firmly spun'

(16:91-92). Both men and women are promised a 'good and pure life' in the Hereafter, provided they do good and righteous works and have faith (16:97). *Āyāt* 98 and 99 enjoin believers to seek refuge from Satan in reading the Qur'ān, as he has no power over true believers. Towards the end, the *sūrah* enjoins believers 'to call men to the path of your Lord with wisdom and kindly exhortation. Reason with them in the most courteous manner.'

17

AL-ISRĀ'

The Night Journey

The *sūrah* derives its title from *āyah* 1, which refers to the Night Journey of the Prophet Muḥammad ﷺ. Revealed at Makkah, and composed of 111 *āyāt,* it is sometimes also called *Banū Isrā'īl,* meaning the Children of Israel, or the Israelites, because of the references made in it to them.

This *sūrah* informs us that Allah has bound the fate of each of us to our neck (17:10). On the Day of Judgement, we will receive an open book to read, which will contain the entire record of the way we passed our life in the world. Rich in content, *ayāt* 23-39 enjoin high moral standards; they particularly emphasise our duties towards our parents: 'Treat them with humility and tenderness and pray: "Lord, forgive them, as they raised me up when I was little"' (17:23-24). People who spend senselessly are called 'brothers of Satan,' (17:27) and adultery is strongly condemned (17:32). *Āyah* 37 enjoins us 'not to walk upon the earth proudly.' Describing the innumerable blessings of Allah upon mankind, it reminds us that Allah guides us by 'land and sea' (17:70). Towards the end, the *sūrah* says that Allah has 'set forth for us in the Qur'ān all manner of arguments,' and that 'if all humans and jinn combined to write the like of this

Qur'ān, they would surely fail to write the like' (17:88). The *sūrah* also contains the prayer: 'Lord, let my entry be by the Gate of Truth and likewise my exit; sustain me with Your power' (17:80). According to ʿĀ'ishah, the Prophet used to recite this *sūrah* every night in his prayer.

18

AL-KAHF

The Cave

The *sūrah* was revealed at Makkah and contains 110 *āyāt*. The title is derived from the narrative about the People of the Cave *(Aṣḥāb al-Kahf)* who, according to the *sūrah*, 'were wonders among Our signs.' The story is intended to confirm faith in the life after death, and the principle of abandoning the world for the sake of faith is deepened into an allegory of death, resurrection and spiritual awakening.

The *sūrah* goes on to relate the parable of two men, one rich and one poor. The rich man behaved as if whatever he possessed was not due to Allah's bounty. When he entered his fruit-laden orchard, instead of being thankful to the Almighty, he said, proudly, 'Surely this will never perish!' The poor man, remonstrating with him for his lack of gratitude, warned him of how the Lord might reward him (the poor man) and punish him (the rich man). Finally the rich man's fruits were destroyed by a rainstorm. This parable is meant to instruct believers never to speak proudly, but to say in all humility, 'Whatever Allah wills will surely come to pass: there is no power save with Allah.' *Āyah* 46 reminds us that 'wealth and children are an adornment of this world's life. But good deeds are better and more lasting, and are better rewarded by your Lord.'

The *sūrah* also tells of the Prophet Mūsā's meeting with al-Khaḍir. The Prophet Mūsā (Moses) عليه السلام was told by Allah to travel towards the 'union of the seas' to meet al-Khaḍir, who was probably an angel in human form, so that he might share some knowledge with him. Mūsā set out with his disciple, Yūshaʿ (Joshua), and ultimately reached the appointed place, where he found al-Khaḍir. Mūsā said to al-Khaḍir: 'May I follow you, so that you may guide me by that which you have been taught?' 'You would not bear with me,' replied al-Khaḍir, 'for how can you bear with that which is beyond your knowledge?'

When Mūsā عليه السلام assured him that he would find him patient, al-Khaḍir let him follow him, reminding him not to question anything until he himself mentioned it. The two then set forth. Al-Khaḍir did several strange things like boring a hole in the boat they were travelling in, killing an innocent boy, and so on. To Mūsā these acts appeared so wicked that he questioned them on each occasion. Ultimately, al-Khaḍir parted with Mūsā, but explained how what he had done was not his will but the order of his Lord, and things were not as they seemed (18:65-82).

The story of al-Khaḍir shows that the manifestation of the highest divine wisdom sometimes takes place in the form of an apparent loss. Man's limited knowledge and his inability to see into the future cause him to feel great concern over what he thinks are tragedies. But a true believer would never lose heart at such losses, for he would know that the beneficent hand of Allah, that works in nature, unceasingly directs humanity towards the goal of the greatest good. This is the lesson which is derived from the story of al-Khaḍir.

The Lord says in *āyah* 54: 'In this Qur'ān, We have set forth for people all manner of parables.' The *sūrah* also tells of Dhu'l Qarnayn, 'the Two-Horned One,' whose story shows that it is not necessary to abstain from worldly life and power in pursuit of spiritual righteousness, so long as we remain conscious of Allah. And the *sūrah* comes to an end with one of the most vivid and powerful passages of the Qur'ān: 'Say: If the sea were ink for the words of my Lord, the sea would indeed dry up before my Lord's words were exhausted, even if We had added another ocean like it, to replenish it' (18:109).

19

MARYAM

Mary

The *sūrah* was revealed at Makkah and contains 98 *āyāt*. The title is taken from the story of Maryam told in *āyāt* 16–35. The *sūrah* begins with a mention of the Prophet Zakariyyā's prayer in which 'he invoked his Lord secretly' for a son who could succeed him. In spite of his old age and his wife being barren, Allah answered his 'secret calling,' sending him the glad tidings of Yaḥyā (John) عليه السلام. The *sūrah* then gives a detailed account of Maryam and the miraculous birth of her son, the Prophet ᶜĪsā (Jesus) عليه السلام, who was Yaḥyā's cousin.

The story concludes with the words of the Prophet ᶜĪsā, which he uttered while yet in his cradle: 'I am the servant of Allah. He has given me the Book, and made me a Prophet. Blessed has He made me wherever I may be; and He has enjoined me to pray and to give alms so long as I live. He has made me kind and dutiful towards my mother, and has not made me arrogant or bereft of grace. Peace be upon me, the day I was born, and the day I shall die, and the day I shall be raised up alive' (19:30–33).

Mentioning the Prophets Ibrāhīm, Mūsā, Ismāᶜīl, Idrīs, Nūḥ, and Isrā'īl, the *sūrah* says that 'when the revelations of the Merciful were recited to them, they fell down on their knees in tears and adoration' (19:58).

The *sūrah* asserts that 'none is there in the heavens or on earth but shall return to the Merciful in utter submission' and that 'every one of them shall come to Him upon the Day of Judgement, all alone' to face their individual judgement (19:93-95). The *sūrah* concludes by saying that Allah has made the Qur'ān easy so that it may give 'good tidings to the godfearing' and 'warnings to the contentious people' (19:97).

20

ṬĀ HĀ

This *sūrah,* consisting of 135 *āyāt,* was revealed in Makkah. Its title is composed of two letters of the Arabic alphabet. The *sūrah* begins by proclaiming: 'We did not reveal the Qur'ān to make you unhappy, but only as an admonition to those who fear (Allah).' This particular portion of the *sūrah* along with some preceding *āyāt* accidently fell into the hands of ʿUmar ibn al-Khaṭṭāb, who until then had been a bitter enemy of the Prophet. Their perusal was sufficient to convert him to Islam. The *sūrah* deals in considerable detail with the story of the Prophet Mūsā عليه السلام in *āyāt* 9-98.

Describing the scene of the Day of Judgement, the *sūrah* tells of the sinners murmuring among themselves: 'You stayed on earth but for ten days,' and the most perceptive among them will declare: 'You stayed there only for a day' (20:104). On that Day the Lord will crush the mountains into fine dust, reducing them to a desolate waste. People will follow their truthful summoner, and 'shall hear only the sound of marching feet.' On that Day there will be no intercession, except with His permission (20:109). The *sūrah* then goes on to urge the believers to pray: 'Lord, increase my knowledge' (20:114) and to 'give glory to your

Lord before sunrise and before sunset. Praise Him in the watches of the night, and the end of the day, so that you may find comfort' (20:130). The *sūrah* concludes by reminding believers not to regard with envy the worldy benefits Allah has bestowed on some people, as through this He seeks only to try them (20:131).

21

AL-ANBIYĀ'

The Prophets

This *sūrah* was revealed at Makkah and contains 112 *āyāt*. It begins by reminding us that the Day of Reckoning is drawing closer, although we may blithely choose to disregard this. It goes on to stress the oneness, uniqueness and transcendence of Allah. *Āyah* 30 describes the creation of the universe in these words: '...the heavens and the earth were joined together in one mass, before We clove them asunder,' and states that Allah has made 'every living thing from water.' These are truths which science has only recently established. A major portion of the *sūrah* is devoted to describing the lives of many prophets, all of whom preached the same fundamental truths.

22

AL-ḤAJJ

The Pilgrimage

The *sūrah* was revealed at Makkah and contains 78 *āyāt*. The title is drawn from *āyāt* 26-30 which provide instruction about the pilgrimage. The *sūrah* begins by warning us about the 'violent convulsion of the Last Hour.' 'When that day comes, every suckling mother shall forsake her infant, every pregnant female shall cast her burden, and you shall see mankind reeling like drunkards, although not drunk.' Then, on the assumption that people may have doubts about the Resurrection, the *sūrah* goes on to recall the stages of the creation of humanity, one by one, later commending the humble among them because their hearts are 'filled with awe at the mention of Allah' (22:35). The *sūrah,* rich in content, describes a unique divine law, through which Allah defends 'some people by the might of others,' failing which 'the monasteries and churches, the synagogues and mosques in which His praise is much celebrated, would have been utterly destroyed' (22:40). The *sūrah* concludes by proclaiming the Muslims the guides of mankind to the true path, just as the Prophet Muḥammad ﷺ is a guide and example for them.

23

AL-MU'MINŪN

The Believers

The *sūrah* was revealed at Makkah and contains 118 *āyāt*. The *sūrah*, as its title indicates, outlines the basis of true faith—faith coupled with humility and diligence in prayer, charity, mindfulness of one's chastity, justness and abstinence from all kinds of vanity (23:1-9). *Āyah* 12 gives a precise description of the creation and development of the human embryo.

Elsewhere the *sūrah* describes true believers as those who pay their *zakāt* with hearts filled with awe (23:60). While mentioning several prophets, the *sūrah* records the prayer of the Prophet Nūḥ عليه السلام when he was saved from the great Flood: 'Lord, let my landing from this ark be blessed. You alone can make me land in safety' (23:29). *Āyāt* 97 and 98 are a prayer to take refuge from the promptings of the devils. The *sūrah* concludes with this prayer: 'Say: Lord, forgive and have mercy. You are the best of those that show mercy' (23:118).

24

AN-NŪR

The Light

This *sūrah*, revealed at Madīnah in 64 *āyāt*. It contains important injunctions on personal and social matters, with special emphasis on family life.

The *sūrah* begins by condemning sex offences for which it prescribes severe punishment—100 lashes each for the adulterer and adulteress, to be administered in public. Four witnesses must, however, be produced to prove the crime. False accusers of chaste women are equally deserving of severe punishment (24:2-4). *Āyāt* 11-16 refers to an incident related to the Prophet's wife, ʿĀ'ishah.

The *sūrah* adds that 'the one that walks in Satan's footsteps is incited to indecency and evil,' (24:21) and urges believers to help their kindred, the poor and those who have migrated for the cause of Allah, even if they had said hurtful or displeasing things: 'Rather let them pardon and forgive. Do you not wish Allah to forgive you?' (24:22). Believers are advised to seek permission before entering someone's house, failing which they should go away (24:27-28). Believing men and believing women are enjoined to 'lower their gaze' and to be mindful of their chastity: 'This will make their lives purer.' Believing women are particularly enjoined to cover their adornments, drawing their veils over their bosoms, and not to reveal their finery except to their husbands, children and close relatives (24:30-31).

The Light of Allah, which gives the *sūrah* its title, is thus described:

> Allah is the Light of the heavens and the earth;
> His Light may be compared to a niche that enshrines a lamp,
> the lamp within a crystal of star-like brilliance.
> It is kindled from a Blessed Tree,
> an olive that is neither of the East nor of the West,
> Whose oil would almost shine forth,
> even before the fire touched it.
> Light upon Light;
> Allah guides to His Light whom He will.
>
> (24:35)

The Light in the above parable denotes Allah's guidance, the niche the heart of a believer, the lamp sincerity of faith, and the glass and oil further strength of faith. The parable suggests that Allah has endowed every human heart with the capacity for true faith in its purest form. The moment the Truth is brought closer to the believer, he will not hesitate to accept it.

True believers are depicted as those whose trade and profits neither divert them from remembrance of Allah, nor from offering prayers and giving alms, as they dread the Day of Judgment when 'peoples hearts and eyes shall be overturned in anguish' (24:37). The *sūrah* uses another strong parable to describe the plight of sinners on that Day: 'Like darkness on a bottomless ocean spread with clashing billows and overcast with clouds: darkness upon darkness. If he (or she) stretches out his hand, he can scarely see it' (24:39-40).

Those unmindful of their Lord are reminded that whatever is in the heavens and in the earth extols Allah's glory, even the birds spreading their wings (24:41). The *sūrah* shows how Allah bends to His will the clouds, rain, lightning, mountains, the day and the night and how every living being is created out of water (24:43-45). 24:58 deals with important aspects of privacy in the family, where the term *ᶜawrah* indicates those parts of a mature person's body which cannot in decency be exposed to any but one's spouse or, in the case of illness, one's doctor. As for personal and family privacy, children should always ask leave to enter parents' and elders' rooms on three occasions: before the morning prayer, in the afternoon and after the night prayer. Before rising in the morning, at siesta time, and after bed-time are the occasions when adults are most likely to be in bed resting.

The *sūrah* lays final stress on mutual charity, compassion, good-fellowship, etiquette and personal modesty.

25

AL-FURQĀN

The Criterion

The *sūrah* (the title of which is also one of the names of the Qur'ān), was revealed at Makkah and contains 77 *āyāt*. It opens with the statement that the Prophet Muḥammad ﷺ has been sent with a divine message for all mankind, the Qur'ān, which provides a criterion for us to distinguish truth from falsehood, right from wrong. It also asserts that those who believe in it and those who do not will not have the same ultimate fate. The *sūrah* then goes on to emphasise the worship of one God. The idol-worshippers will be assembled by Allah along with what they worshipped and He will ask them: 'Was it you who misled My servants, or did they choose to go astray?' They will answer that it was the comforts of this life which made them forget the warning (25:17-18). On that Day the sinner will bite his hands, saying: 'Would that I had walked in the Messenger's path' (25:27). The Prophet Muḥammad ﷺ will also complain on that Day to Allah that his people have forsaken the Qur'ān (25:30).

The *sūrah* also points to the person 'who makes his own desires his deity' (25:42). Decrying such a person, the Prophet warns that, in the sight of Allah, the most heinous form of idol-worship under the sun is the following of one's own desires (aṭ-Ṭabarānī). Believers are asked to perform *jihād kabīr* with the help of the Holy Qur'ān: 'By means of this (Qur'ān), strive with them, most strenuously' (25:52). Peaceful *daʿwah* work is cited here as a form of true *jihād*.

The *sūrah* concludes with a vivid description of the true servants of Allah.

26
ASH-SHUʿARĀ’
The Poets

The *sūrah* was revealed at Makkah and contains 227 *āyāt*. *Āyah* 224, from which the title is taken, disparages poets as not being sincere portrayers of reality. *Āyāt* 192-195 explain how the Qur’ān was revealed in plain Arabic by the Lord of the Universe, and that the ‘faithful spirit’ (Jibrīl) brought it down to the heart of the Prophet, so that mankind might be warned by it.

The *sūrah* begins by counselling the Prophet Muḥammad ﷺ not to ‘fret himself to death’ on account of people’s rejection of his call to Truth. This anxiety on the part of the Prophet indicates to what degree a *dāʿī* of Truth is sincere towards his audience. Such sincerity is also required of true believers towards their *madʿū*.

A major portion of the *sūrah* narrates the histories of several prophets of the past, and the many-sided, many-layered lessons to be drawn from their lives and teachings. These prophets include Mūsā, Ibrāhīm, Nūḥ, Hūd, Ṣāliḥ, Lūṭ and Shuʿayb, upon all of whom be peace. Narrating the story of the Prophet Mūsā عليه السلام, the *sūrah* describes how the armies of the Firʿawn (Pharaoh) chased the Banū Isrā’īl, who were led by the Prophet Mūsā عليه السلام out of Egypt. They felt utterly helpless and lamented loudly to Mūsā: 'We are surely undone.' But the Prophet Mūsā at that dreaded moment showed no sign of worry, and only said, 'My Lord is with me, and He will guide me' (26:62). This faith and confidence in the Almighty is desired of every true believer in moments of distress.

Āyāt 78-82 introduce the divine attributes of the Lord of the universe, who creates human beings, who gives guidance, food and drink. When people are sick, it is He who restores them to good health. Allah will cause us to die, but will bring us back to life in the Hereafter. The *sūrah* then proceeds to a long prayer. The phrase 'Surely in that there was a sign, yet most of them do not believe,' is repeated eight times.

27

AN-NAML

The Ant

The *sūrah* was revealed at Makkah and contains 93 *āyāt*. The title of the *sūrah* is taken from *āyāt* 18 and 19, which recount how the Prophet Sulaymān (Solomon) عليه السلام and his armies were passing through a valley inhabited by ants. Seeing the soldiers, one ant cried out, 'Quick, get out of the way and hide! Sulaymān and his soldiers will trample on us...!' Sulaymān عليه السلام was so gifted as to understand the speech of ants. He smiled, therefore, and let the ants move to one side.

The *sūrah* begins by asserting that the revelations of the Qur'ān are 'a guide and glad tidings to the true believers.' It goes on to narrate the stories of earlier prophets such as Mūsā, Sulaymān, Ṣāliḥ and Lūṭ, upon all of whom be peace. *Āyah* 40 asserts that property and grace are basically given to us to test us, to reveal whether we show gratefulness to Allah.

Āyah 82 warns that a time will come when a beast (*dābbah*) will come out of the earth and will speak to the people. According to a *ḥadīth,* this shall be a sign of the approach of the Last Day. Before the present world passes away, Allah will bring forth extraordinary signs. One of these signs will be this creature. Those who did not respond to the call of human warners, will listen to the call of Truth from a non-human creature. But this will be the announcement of the end of the time for testing, not of its beginning...

The *sūrah* ends with the warning that on the Day when the Trumpet is sounded, mountains which have always seemed firm will pass away like clouds, and 'those who shall come with good deeds, shall be rewarded with what is better, and shall be secure from the terrors of that Day. But those who come with evil deeds shall be hurled headlong into the Fire' (27: 89-90).

28

AL-QAṢAṢ

The Story

This *sūrah* was revealed at Makkah and contains 88 *āyāt*. It is chiefly devoted to the story of the Prophet Mūsā عليه السلام from the time of his birth to his exile in Madyan, and from his subsequent receiving of the prophethood to the time when he led the Banū Isrā'īl out of Egypt.

The *sūrah* then deals with the message brought by the Prophet Muḥammad عليه السلام, which was recognized by those who knew the earlier revelation, although by accepting a new religion they had to suffer in different ways. Thus they received a two-fold reward from Allah, because they 'endured with fortitude, requiting evil with good' (28:54).

The *sūrah* also narrates the story of Qārūn (Korah) who accumulated so much wealth that the keys to his treasures were too difficult even for several strong men to carry (28:76). Instead of being grateful to Allah, he chose to be tyrannical and overbearing. His people admonished him and asked him to spend on charity and good works. But he behaved arrogantly, arguing that the wealth which he possessed was due to his own knowledge and cleverness. When he publicly displayed the glitter of his immense wealth, 'Allah caused the earth to engulf him and his palace'

(28:82). Seeing the terrible end to which Qārūn came, 'those who on the day before had longed to be in his position began to say: "Behold! Allah gives abundantly to whom He will and sparingly to whom He pleases"' (28:83). Thus the exemplary punishment of Qārūn is a great reminder to the believers to be grateful to Allah and to thank Him both in times of abundance and times of poverty.

The *sūrah* concludes with the invocations that 'there is no deity save Allah' and that 'all things shall perish except Himself' (28:88).

29

AL-ᶜANKABŪT

The Spider

The *sūrah* was revealed at Makkah and contains 69 *āyāt*. The title is derived from *āyah* 41 which likens the false gods from whom people seek help, to the spider's cobweb, the weakest of all dwellings. The *sūrah* begins by declaring that simply stating, 'We are believers' is not enough. Every soul shall be put to the test. The *sūrah* goes on to narrate the stories of a number of prophets, which are full of lessons and admonitions. *Āyah* 45 reminds the believers to be steadfast in prayer, as this 'forbids indecency and evil.' The *sūrah* then goes on to deal with life after death, the creation of the heavens and the earth, the distribution of sustenance to every creature on earth, and concludes by reminding man that the 'life of this world is but a sport and a pastime. It is the life to come that is the true life' (29:64).

30

AR-RŪM

The Byzantines

The *sūrah* of 60 *āyāt,* revealed at Makkah, in 616 A.D. (seven years before the *hijrah*) takes its title from the prophecy to the Romans.

Its central theme is the signs in nature of Allah's creation (*āyāt* 20–25): man created from dust, marriage, so that men may live in peace with women (thus Allah imbued our hearts with love and mercy) the heavens and earth, the variations in languages and colours of the human race, sleeping at night and the quest for His bounty by day, lightning and rainfall.

It warns that if 'evil has become rife on land and sea,' it is 'in consequence of humanity's misdeeds' (30:41). Believers are urged to be firm in the true faith and to preserve, uncorrupted, the 'upright nature' with which we have been created (30:30). Usurers are condemned, whereas charity given for His sake 'will surely be repaid many times over' (30:39).

The *sūrah* contains the only specific mention in the Qur'ān (*āyāt* 17 and 18) of the five daily prayers or *ṣalāt*.

It concludes by exhorting believers to endure with patience and fortitude, for Allah's promise is true.

31

LUQMĀN

The *sūrah* was revealed at Makkah and contains 34 *āyāt*. It begins by stating that the Qur'ān is a book full of wisdom, a guide and a blessing to the righteous, who are regular in prayers, pay *zakāt*, and firmly believe in the life Hereafter.

The sage Luqmān, after whom the sūrah is named, wisely counsels his son: 'O my son, serve no other deity beside Allah; for idolatry is an abominable sin. (We enjoined people to show kindness to their parents, for with much pain their mothers bear them, and they are not weaned before they are two years of age. We said: "Be thankful to Me and to your parents. To Me shall all things return. But if they press you to serve besides Me deities you know nothing of, do not obey them. Be kind to them in this world, and follow the path of those who turn to Me. To Me you shall all return, and I will declare to you all that you have done.") O my son, Allah will bring all things to light, be they as small as a grain of mustard seed, be they hidden inside a rock or in heaven or earth. Gracious is Allah and All-knowing. O my son, be steadfast in prayer, enjoin justice, and forbid dishonour. Endure with fortitude whatever befalls you. That is a duty incumbent on all. Do not treat people with scorn, nor walk proudly on the earth: Allah does not love the arrogant and the vainglorious. Rather let your gait be modest and your voice low; the harshest of voices is the braying of the ass' (31:13-19).

Total submission to the will of Allah is termed 'the firmest bond' (31:22). To express the unimaginable vastness of Allah's creations, the *sūrah* aptly declares: 'If all the trees on earth were pens, and the sea, replenished by seven more seas, were ink, the words of Allah would not be exhausted' (31:27). The *sūrah* concludes by reminding us of the awe of the Day of Judgement, when we are judged for ourselves without any loved one to make excuses for us, 'when no parent shall avail his child, nor any child his parent' (31:33).

32
AS-SAJDAH
Prostration

The *sūrah* was revealed at Makkah and contains 30 *āyāt*. The title is taken from *āyah* 15, in which the believers are described as falling down prostrate when the divine messages are revealed to them. The *sūrah* asserts that this Qur'ān is a direct revelation from the Almighty, and goes on to describe Allah's creative power and might:

> Allah is He that created the heavens and the earth,
> and what is between them, in six days,
> then seated Himself upon the Throne.
> Apart from Him, you have neither protector
> nor mediator; will you not take heed?
> He governs all from heaven to earth.
> And all will ascend to Him in a single day, whose
> measure is a thousand years of your reckoning.
> He is the knower of the Unseen and the Visible,
> the All-mighty, the All-compassionate,
> Who excelled in the creation of all things.
> He first created man from clay,
> then He fashioned his progeny from a drop of
> humble fluid. Then He shaped him, and breathed
> His spirit into him.
> He gave you eyes and ears and hearts:
> yet you are seldom thankful.
>
> (32:4–9)

33

AL-AḤZĀB

The Confederates

The *sūrah* was revealed at Madīnah and contains 73 *āyāt*. The title of the *sūrah* refers to those tribes who, along with the Makkan Quraysh, besieged Madīnah in the 5th year of the Hijrah. Avoiding a direct confrontation, the Prophet Muḥammad ﷺ had a trench dug, which effectively prevented the enemy onslaught on the city. The rest of the *sūrah* deals with the Prophet's family life and draws the attention of believers to certain rules of conduct in their domestic relations.

34

SABĀ'

Sheba

The *sūrah* was revealed at Makkah and contains 54 *āyāt*. The title is based on the reference to the people of Saba' in the Yemen. Reference is also made to the Prophets Dāwūd عليه السلام and Sulaymān عليه السلام and their superior knowledge of things hidden from us. The plants, mountains and birds used to sing in praise of Allah along with Dāwūd (34:10). Sulaymān was acquainted with the speech of birds and animals. Unseen forces, such as devils and jinn were assigned to work for him (21:82; 34:13). Moreover the raging wind 'sped at his command' (21:81). Allah also taught him the use of iron, and a fountain of molten brass was made to flow for his benefit.

To those who deny the reality of resurrection and life after death, the *sūrah* poses the question: 'Are they, then, not aware of how little of the sky and the earth lies open before them, and how much is hidden from them?' (34:9). Then how can we, with our limited knowledge, deny the reality of resurrection?

Towards its end, the *sūrah* enjoins: 'I counsel you one thing only: Be ever conscious of standing before Allah, whether in the company of others or alone' (34:46).

35

AL-FĀṬIR

The Creator

The *sūrah* was revealed at Makkah and contains 45 *āyāt*. The title is taken from *āyah* 1, which opens by praising Allah, the Creator and Sustainer of the heavens and the earth. The main theme of the *sūrah* is Allah's unique power of creation and resurrection. The angels are called 'messengers with wings' (35:1), who unceasingly carry out the task assigned to them and maintain the vast universe with the utmost precision. To explain Allah's might and majesty, the *sūrah* goes on to give some examples of His creations such as the fresh and sweet water of rivers and ponds and the salty and bitter water of the sea; the gems, pearls and coral that we take from the sea and also the fresh fish; ships that sail thereon; and the phenomena of day and night, and sun and moon. All these things are pressed into the service of humanity, but some in their heedlessness invoke powerless idols (35:12-14) and do not ever ponder that it is Allah alone who keeps the heavens and the earth from falling. Should they fall, none could hold them back but He (35:41).

The *sūrah* concludes by declaring that had it been the Almighty's will to punish people for their misdeeds, not one creature would be left alive on earth. But Allah gives respite till the Day of Judgement.

36
YĀ SĪN

This *sūrah*, whose title consists of two letters of the Arabic alphabet, *yā* and *sīn*, was revealed at Makkah and contains 83 *āyāt*. It opens with a statement that the Qur'ān is a book full of wisdom, a Revelation sent down by the Merciful, so that people may heed its warnings. Later the *sūrah* asserts that the Qur'ān is not poetry. It is revealed in plain language to 'exhort the living and to pass judgement on the unbelievers' (36:69–70).

The *sūrah* describes the signs of Allah in nature, such as things created in pairs, the plants, living things, the night and day, the sun and the moon, and so on. The revolution of the sun in space (36:38) and the movement of the heavenly bodies in their orbits (36:40) are recently discovered scientific facts, which were not known to man 1400 years ago. This amply proves the divine nature of the Qur'ān.

The *sūrah* then goes on to deal with the Resurrection, when the Trumpet shall be blown, and the dead will rise up from their graves, saying: 'Woe betide us! Who has roused us from our resting place?' But it will be a single blast, and everyone shall be gathered before Allah (36:49). On that Day no soul shall suffer the least injustice. All will be rewarded for their own deeds.

'On that Day We shall seal their mouths. Their hands will speak to Us, and their very feet will testify to their misdeeds' (36:65).

The *sūrah,* which concludes by reaffirming the certainty of resurrection, is also called 'the heart of the Qur'ān.'

37

AṢ-ṢĀFFĀT

Those Ranged in Ranks

This *sūrah* was revealed at Makkah and contains 182 *āyāt*. Its title is taken from the beginning of the first *āyah:* 'By those who range themselves in ranks,' meaning the ranks of angels in front of Allah. The *sūrah* stresses the Oneness of Allah (37:4) and goes on to stress the certainty of the resurrection and the Day of Judgement as well as the torment of Hell and the delights of Paradise. Stories of the Prophets Nūḥ, Ibrāhīm, Mūsā, Hārūn, Ilyās, Lūṭ and Yūnus are recounted in quick succession. The Prophet Ibrāhīm's prayer: 'Lord grant me a righteous son' is mentioned in 37:100, and subsequently his 'great sacrifice.' The *sūrah* goes on to deal with the subject of angels and jinn at length and concludes by saying: 'Peace be on the prophets, and praise to Allah, Lord of the Universe' (37:182).

38

ṢĀD

The title of this *sūrah* is taken from the letter *ṣ* (*ṣād*) of the Arabic alphabet, which is prefixed to the *sūrah*. It contains 88 *āyāt* and was revealed at Makkah during the social boycott of the Prophet Muḥammad ﷺ and his family by the Quraysh. At that time the Prophet was frequently scorned as 'a sorcerer, a teller of lies' (38:4). The *sūrah* counsels him, therefore, to 'have patience at what they say' (38:65). It goes on to relate at some length the stories of the Prophet Dāwūd and Sulaymān, and mentions a number of other prophets such as Ayyūb, Ibrāhīm, Ishāq, Yāʿqūb, Ismāʿīl, Alyasaʿ and Dhu'l-Kifl. The *sūrah* also deals with the subject of the angels and Satan (Iblīs), Hell and Heaven, and concludes by reaffirming that the Qur'ān is an admonition to mankind.

39
AZ-ZUMAR
The Throngs

The *sūrah* was revealed at Makkah and contains 75 *āyāt*. The title is taken from *āyāt* 71 and 73 which refer to the two groups of believers and non-believers which will be formed on the Day of Judgement. The group of unbelievers will be driven down to Hell, while the believing group will be ushered towards Paradise. The main themes of the *sūrah* are Allah's oneness, His existence, the certainty of the Resurrection and powerful condemnation of *shirk* (polytheism).

The *sūrah* begins by announcing that the Qur'ān is revealed 'with the truth,' therefore, one should worship his Lord with the sincere faith which is rightly due to Him. It further asserts the might of Allah, who 'created the heavens and the earth; caused the night and day to succeed each other and made the sun and the moon obedient to Him, each running for an appointed time set by the Mighty, the Benign One.' (39:5). Enjoining people to be grateful to their Lord, the *sūrah* observes: 'Can the one who passes the night in adoration, standing or kneeling, who dreads the terrors of the life to come and hopes to earn the mercy of the Lord, be compared to the unbeliever?' (39:9). The Qur'ān is called 'the fairest teaching' proclaiming promises and warnings: 'Those who fear their Lord tremble with awe at its revelations, and their skins and hearts melt at the remembrance of Allah' (39:23). The Qur'ān is further described as a book 'free from any flaw,' containing 'all manner of parables, so that they may take heed' (39:27-28). The *sūrah* goes on to counsel the believers:

> Say: 'Servants of Allah, you that have sinned against your souls, do not despair of Allah's mercy, for He forgives all sins. It is He who is the Forgiving One, the Merciful' (39:53).

The *sūrah* laments that people, being ignorant of Allah, do not honour their Lord as is His due. On the Day of Resurrection Allah will hold the entire earth in His grasp and fold up the heavens in His right hand (39:67) and the angels will circle around the Throne of the Almighty giving glory to Him. Vividly picturing the happenings of the Day of Judgement, the *sūrah* says, in conclusion, that, those who are awarded Paradise will say: 'Praise be to Allah, Lord of the Universe!' (39:75).

40

AL-MU'MIN

The Believer

This *sūrah* of 85 *āyāt,* also called *Ghāfir,* or 'Forgiving,' which was revealed at Makkah. Its title is taken from *āyāt* 28-45, in which the believing relative of Fir[c]awn (Pharaoh) speaks out in favour of Mūsā ﷺ. It begins by mentioning a number of Divine attributes: 'This Book is revealed by Allah, the Mighty One, the All-knowing, who forgives sin and accepts repentance. His punishment is stern but His bounty infinite. There is no god but Allah. All shall return to Him.' The main theme of the *sūrah* is the Divine power and His great planning in the universe. After a brief mention of the Prophet Nūḥ ﷺ, the *sūrah* tells at length of the angels, bearing the Throne and standing around it, giving glory to and praising their Lord. They implore Allah to forgive the believers, saying, 'Admit them, Lord, to the gardens of Eden which you have promised them, together with all the righteous among their fathers, their spouses, and their descendants' (40:8). Depicting the approach of the Last Day, the *sūrah* warns that on that Day, people's hearts will leap up to their throats, choking them, and that the sinner will find neither friend nor intercessor. Therefore, the *sūrah* urges believers to beg forgiveness for their sins, and to praise their Lord evening and morning, as their Lord has said: 'Call on Me and I shall respond to you' (40:60). The *sūrah* goes on to mention a number of Allah's blessings and bounties, and concludes by asking, 'Which of Allah's signs do you deny?' (40:81).

41
FUṢṢILAT
Revelations Well Expounded

The *sūrah*, composed of 54 *āyāt* and revealed at Makkah, is also called *Ḥā Mīm Sajdah.* It begins by announcing that the Qur'ān is revealed by the Compassionate, the Merciful: 'a Book of revelations well expounded, an Arabic Qur'ān for people of knowledge.' After dealing with the creation of the heavens and the earth and relating the stories of ʿĀd and Thamūd, the *sūrah* explains how, on Judgment Day, our own skins will speak out against us: 'Their eyes, their ears, and their very skins will testify to their misdeeds. "Why did you speak against us?" they would say to their skins, and their skins would reply: "Allah who gives speech to all things, has made us speak. It was He who in the beginning created you, and to Him you shall be recalled. You did not hide yourselves, so that your eyes and ears and skins could not be made to testify against you. Yet you thought that Allah did not know much of what you did. It was the thoughts you entertained about your Lord that ruined you, so that you are now among the lost."'

(Modern scientific research suggests that human skin is capable of recording and replaying messages. This is called 'skin-speech.')

Angels are said to descend to the righteous and

they counsel them, saying: 'We are your guardians in this world and in the Hereafter' (41:31). Believers are urged to call others to Allah, and to do what is right (41:33). Giving a golden rule for mutual harmony, the *sūrah* says: 'Good and evil are not alike. Repel evil with good, and he, between whom and you there is enmity, will become your dearest friend.'

The dead earth being revived by rain is compared with the life after death (41:39-40). The Qur'ān acts for believers as a guide and a healing balm (41:44). *Āyah* 47 says that no fruit is borne, and no female concieves or is delivered, but with His knowledge.

Depicting human ingratitude, the *sūrah* says that when evil befalls us, we lose hope and grow despondent, but when Allah vouchsafes us—His favours, we say: 'This is my due' (41:50).

The *sūrah* concludes with the following passage: We will show them Our signs in the universe and in their own selves, until it becomes clear to them that this (Qur'ān) is indeed the truth (41:53).

The above *āyah* is the prediction that what is laid down in the Qur'ān is the ultimate truth, which will be borne out by all future knowledge

42
ASH-SHŪRĀ
Consultation

The *sūrah*, which contains 35 *āyāt,* was revealed at Makkah. Its title is taken from *āyah* 38, which calls for *shūrā baynahum* (mutual consent), this being the basic social principle which ought to characterize any community of true believers.

The *sūrah* begins by naming several divine attributes—the Mighty One, the Wise, Most High, the Supreme, and goes on to stress the reality of divine revelation, asking the Prophet, and through him all believers, to propagate its message (42:7). After a brief mention of the Prophets Nūḥ, Ibrāhīm, Mūsā and ʿĪsā, the *sūrah* goes on to describe the Hour of Doom. 'Those who deny it... seeking the harvest of this world, a share of it shall be theirs. But in the hereafter they shall have no share at all' (42:19-20).

Allah accepts the repentance of His servants... and answers those who have faith and do good works, and enriches them through His bounty (42:24-25). *Āyah* 30 says whatever calamity befalls man is 'the outcome of what his hands have wrought.' *Āyāt* 37-43 define true believers in terms of their desirable characteristics:

> Those who avoid gross sins and indecencies and, when angered, are willing to forgive, who obey their

> Lord, attend to their prayers and conduct their affairs by mutual consultation, who bestow in alms a part of what We have given them and, when tyranny afflicts them, defend themselves (42:37-39).

When sinners 'face the scourge, they will exclaim: "Is there no way back?"' But 'the wrongdoers will suffer everlasting torment' (42:44-46). The *sūrah* concludes by reaffirming that the Prophet Muḥammad ﷺ is guiding us to the right path—'the path of Allah, to whom belongs all that the heavens and the earth contain. Surely to Allah all things shall in the end return.'

43
AZ-ZUKHRUF
The Ornaments of Gold

The *sūrah* was revealed at Makkah and contains 89 *āyāt*. Its title is taken from *āyah* 35 which states that worldly things such as gold and silver keep people away from the Truth.

The *sūrah* begins by proclaiming the divine origin of the Qur'ān which was revealed in Arabic (i.e. in a human language) so that people might understand its meaning, though the original book remains in the keeping of Allah. In the spirit of gratefulness, and citing our utter weakness, the *sūrah* urges us to pray while riding on the back of an animal, or boarding a ship: 'Glory be to Him who has subjected these to us, we ourselves could not be their masters. To our Lord we shall all return' (43:13). The Prophet habitually recited this prayer while riding his horse or camel.

According to this *sūrah*, one who does not heed the warning of the Qur'ān, 'shall have a devil for his companion.' On the Day of Judgement such people will cry out, 'Would that we were as far apart as the East is from the West' (43:38). The Prophets Ibrāhīm, Mūsā and ʿĪsā are mentioned, while great stress is laid on the Prophet ʿĪsā عليه السلام being a human being: 'He was no more than a mortal whom We favoured and made an example to the Banū Isrā'īl' (43:59).

Those of Allah's servants who have believed in His revelations and surrendered themselves to Him will have nothing to fear on the Day of Judgement. They will be told: 'Enter Paradise, you and your spouses, in all delight' (43:70); while, on the other hand, the evil-doers will endure such a torment that they will cry out to Mālik, one of Hell's keepers, to let the Lord make an end of them. But the answer will be, 'Here you shall remain!' (43:77). The *sūrah* concludes by mentioning a number of divine attributes and asking the Prophet to bear with the unbelievers and wish them peace.

44

AD-DUKHĀN

Smoke

The *sūrah*, which contains 59 *āyāt,* was revealed at Makkah. Its title is taken from *āyah* 10 which says that on the Day of Judgement the sky will pour down visible smoke which will envelop all people. The *sūrah* begins by Allah swearing by the Qur'ān—the Glorious Book—that He revealed it on a blessed night to forewarn mankind. The *sūrah* goes on to deal with the story of the Prophet Mūsā عليه السلام, describing the evil fate of Fir'awn and his people: 'How many gardens, how many fountains they left behind them! Cornfields, and noble palaces, and good things in which they took delight. All this they left; and what was once theirs We gave to other people. Neither heaven nor earth shed tears for them' (44:25-29).

Similar references are made to the people of Tubba' (the people of Himyar, in Arabia), the creation of heaven and earth and the *zaqqūm* tree of Hell. The *sūrah* goes on to describe the delights of Paradise and anguish of Hell, and concludes by asserting that the sole purpose of the Qur'ān being revealed is that people may take heed.

45

AL-JĀTHIYAH

The Kneeling Down

The *sūrah*, which contains 37 *āyāt,* was revealed at Makkah. Its title is taken from *āyah* 28, which refers to the kneeling down of all humanity on the Day of Judgement before Almighty Allah.

The *sūrah* begins by announcing that the Qur'ān is revealed by Allah, the Mighty One, the All-knowing, and goes on to describe His signs in our own creation, in the beasts, in night and day, in the rain and winds—all are signs for true believers. The *sūrah* goes on to remind us how Allah has subdued and subjected to mankind 'what the heavens and earth contain' so that people may seek His bounty, and render thanks to Him. All this presents signs for thinking people.

46

AL-AḤQĀF

The Sand Dunes

This *sūrah* of 34 *āyāt* revealed at Makkah, derives its title from *āyah* 21, which refers to al-Aḥqāf, a long tract of sand dunes in Ḥaḍramawt, Yemen, the country of the ᶜĀd people to whom the Prophet Hūd was sent. The ᶜĀd were destroyed for their disbelief.

Emphasis is laid on duties towards parents, failing which one will earn Allah's displeasure: 'We have enjoined man to show kindness to his parents. His mother bore him painfully, and painfully she gave birth to him; he is born and weaned in thirty months. When he grows to manhood and attains his fortieth year, let him say: "Inspire me, Lord, to give thanks for the blessings You have bestowed on me and my parents"' (46:15). This *sūrah* also mentions how the jinn, having listened to the Qur'ān while the Prophet Muḥammad ﷺ was praying, immediately became believers, and hastened back to give its message to their people (46:29-32). Every believer in the Qur'ān is required to become its exponent. The *sūrah* concludes by asking the Prophet Muḥammad ﷺ to show patience towards his audience, like the previous messengers of high resolve. This *sunnah* of the Prophet should be followed by all Muslims when dealing with their *madᶜū* (non-Muslims exposed to the teachings of Islam).

47
MUḤAMMAD

The *sūrah* was revealed at Madīnah and contains 38 *āyāt*. This title is taken from the mention of the Prophet Muḥammad ﷺ in *āyah* 2. The *sūrah* gives considerable attention to several aspects of defensive fighting (*qitāl*) and emphasises that war captives should be freed unconditionally, or after giving ransom (47:4).

In a touching description of Paradise, the *sūrah* says that there the believer will find rivers of water, milk, honey and wine (47:15). *Āyah* 18 warns of the approach of the Hour of Doom, portents of which have already been made manifest. Believers are enjoined to implore Allah to forgive their sins (47:19). The *sūrah* goes on to deal with the hostile attitude of the hypocrites, saying that Allah will ultimately reveal all the malice they have towards believers (47:29). It also asserts that Allah will test all individuals on their readiness to make sacrifices for His cause (47:31). It concludes by urging us to obey Allah and His Messenger, and cautions that 'the life of this world is but a sport and a pastime.' It promises that those who believe and guard themselves against evil will be richly rewarded.

48
AL-FATḤ
Victory

The *sūrah*, which contains 29 *āyāt,* was revealed at Madīnah. The title is taken from the main theme of the *sūrah,* 'the clear victory' of the Peace Treaty of al-Ḥudaybiyyah.

The Prophet Muḥammad ﷺ is referred to as one who was sent by Allah as a witness, a bearer of good news and a warner (48:8). The *sūrah* goes on to deal mainly with several aspects of the Peace Treaty, especially the excuses of the hypocrites, the steadfastness of the faithful believers and the distribution of booty. It concludes with a very striking passage about the Companions of the Prophet Muḥammad ﷺ: 'Those who follow him are firm and unyielding to the unbelievers but full of mercy to one another. You see them adoring on their knees, seeking the grace of Allah and His good will. Their marks are on their faces, the traces of their prostration...'

49

AL-ḤUJURĀT

The Chambers

The *sūrah* was revealed at Madīnah and contains 18 *āyāt*. It deals mainly with social ethics and teaches good manners and morals. The title is taken from an incident in which a group of the Banū Tamīm tribe visited the Prophet's Mosque in Madīnah and called out to him rudely from behind his private chambers. Thereupon the *sūrah* was revealed.

The *sūrah* cautions believers 'not to raise your voices over the voice of the Prophet, lest your labours should come to nothing without your perceiving it' (49:2). Though this was a commandment for the early Muslims in the Prophet's lifetime, the same applies today to the message brought by the Prophet. Personal opinions and predilections must not be allowed to overrule the clear-cut stipulations of the Qur'ān and Ḥadīth, or those raising their voices, will surely find that in the eyes of Allah their labours have been in vain.

The *sūrah* goes on to say that you should not be carried away by any rumour, but should 'inquire first into its truth, lest you should wrong others unwittingly' (49:6). Of the true believers, the *sūrah* says that 'Allah has endeared the faith to you and beautified it in your hearts, making unbelief, wrongdoing, and disobedience abhorrent to you' (49:7).

Calling the believers 'brothers,' the *sūrah* urges them to make peace between warring Muslim parties, as 'Allah loves those who exercise justice' (49:9–10). We are urged not to mock others, for those others may perhaps be better than ourselves. Defaming others and calling one another by nicknames is likewise condemned. Believers are also asked to avoid immoderate suspicion and spying. Backbiting is likened to eating the flesh of one's own brother (49:11–12).

Shortly before its conclusion, the *sūrah* outlines the basis for the brotherhood of the whole of humanity:

> O humanity, We have created you from a male and a female,
> and made you nations and tribes, so that you may know each other.
> The noblest of you in the sight of Allah is he who is most righteous.
> Allah is all-knowing and wise.
>
> (49:13).

50
QĀF

The *sūrah* was revealed at Makkah and contains 49 *āyāt.* The main emphasis of the *sūrah* is on the certainty of resurrection and the life hereafter. The opening *āyah* is an invocation: '*Qāf.* By the glorious Qur'ān.' (*Qāf* is a letter of the Arabic alphabet.)

After mentioning the doubts of the unbelievers about the resurrection and the prophethood of the Prophet Muḥammad ﷺ, the *sūrah* goes on to describe the wonders of nature such as the skies with their limitless stars and planets, the vast earth spread out with mountains standing firmly thereon and 'all kinds of delectable plants.' All this is calculated to arouse a sense of awe in anyone who truly turns to the Almighty (50:6-8). *Āyāt* 12-15 mentions many disbelieving nations of the past who were destroyed by Allah because of their rejection of His prophets. Elsewhere the *sūrah* says that it is a 'lesson for every man who has a heart, and can hear and see' (50:37).

Allah, according to this *sūrah*, is closer to a person 'than his (or her) own jugular vein,' knows the innermost thoughts of our souls; each word we utter is noted down by two guardian angels, one seated on our right and the other on our left (50:16-18). Depicting the vastness of Hell, the *sūrah* says that on the Day of Judgement Allah will ask Hell, 'Are you full?' And Hell will answer: 'Are there any more?' (50:30). It expands as necessary. No sinner should misguidedly hope he or she might escape because it is full.

The *sūrah* states that Allah created the heavens and the earth and all that lies between them in six days, but that this did not cause Him any sense of weariness (50:38). This is a correction of an interpolation in the present Bible, which says that God created the heavens and earth in six days and 'rested' on the seventh day (Genesis, ii. 3). The Qur'ān also stresses elsewhere that a 'day' does not mean our 24-hour day, dependent on the prior existence of sun, moon and earth. A 'day' is a period or aeon as long as Allah wills.

Believers are then enjoined to praise their Lord before sunrise and before sunset and also at night in prayer and prostration (50:39-40). Reaffirming the certainty of the Last Day, the *sūrah* says that 'when the crier (the angel Isrā'fīl) will call from near; the Day when men will hear the fateful cry, on that Day they will rise up from their graves' (50:41-44).

The *sūrah* concludes by enjoining the Prophet Muḥammad ﷺ—and through him every true believer: 'Admonish with the Qur'ān whoever fears My warning' (50:45).

51

ADH-DHĀRIYĀT

The Winds

The *sūrah* was revealed at Makkah and contains 60 *āyāt.* The title is derived from *āyah* 1. This *sūrah* depicts the righteous who shall dwell amidst gardens and fountains. 'For they have done good works, sleeping but little in the night-time, praying at dawn for (Allah's) forgiveness and sharing their possessions with the beggars and the deprived' (51:15-19). The *sūrah* goes on to tell the stories of the Prophets Ibrāhīm عليه السلام and Mūsā عليه السلام and the peoples of ʿĀd and Thamūd. It then refers to the creation of Allah and describes how Allah created everything in pairs (51:49). The *sūrah* concludes by describing the purpose of creation in very emphatic terms: 'I have only created the jinn and mankind to worship Me' (51:46).

AṬ-ṬŪR
Mount Sinai

The *sūrah* was revealed at Makkah and contains 49 *āyāt*. The title is taken from the opening *āyah* which refers to Mount Sinai as the place where the Prophet Mūsā عليه السلام received Allah's revelation and saw the reflection of His glory (7:143).

The *sūrah* opens with a powerful reference to Allah's signs, such as the high mountains, the vast sky and the swelling sea. All these creations are silent reminders to us that we cannot escape from the Almighty's grip. The prophets all announced the same awesome message through their revelations. Hence the *sūrah* warns, 'Your Lord's punishment shall surely come to pass! No power shall ward it off' (52:7-8). Depicting the scene of the Last Day, the *sūrah* goes on to say: 'On that Day the heaven will shake and reel, and mountains move and pass away. On that Day woe betide the unbelievers, who now divert themselves with vain disputes' (52:9-12). Asserting that 'each person is the hostage of his (or her) own deeds,' the *sūrah* says that the true believers and their descendants, who follow them in their faith, will be united in Paradise (52:21). The *sūrah* then counsels the Prophet Muḥammad ﷺ—and through him every true believer—to warn people of the Last Day (52:29). It goes on to reflect upon why people do not believe: 'Were they created out of nothing? Or were they their own creators? Did *they* create the heavens and the earth? Surely they have no faith' (52:35-36). After describing the hostile behaviour of the unbelievers, the *sūrah* counsels the Prophet to 'wait the judgement of your Lord: We are watching over you' (52:48).

The *sūrah* concludes by urging believers to celebrate and praise the Lord at all times, especially at dawn and at night.

53

AN-NAJM

The Star

The *sūrah* was revealed at Makkah and contains 62 *āyāt*. The title is taken from the invocation in the first *āyah*: 'By the star as it sets.' The *sūrah* opens by asserting that the revelation of the Qur'ān was directly from the Almighty and was brought to the Prophet Muḥammad ﷺ by the angel Jibrīl. The Prophet's Night Journey (*isrā'*) is also mentioned here.

The *sūrah* then describes three goddesses of pre-Islamic Arabia, who were considered to be daughters of God. Condemning this fiction, the *sūrah* says, 'they are just names which people have devised' (53:19-23). *Āyah* 32 says that the Lord, 'abounding in forgiveness,' will forgive the small offenses of those who avoid the grossest sins and indecencies. *Āyāt* 36-44 describe how the teachings of the Qur'ān are the same as those given to the earlier prophets.

The *sūrah* goes on to mention several prophets, and concludes by asserting that the Prophet Muḥammad ﷺ brings a warning and that the Day of Doom is drawing nearer: 'Thus prostrate yourself before Allah and worship Him' (53:62).

54

AL-QAMAR

The Moon

This is an early Makkan *sūrah*, revealed in the 4th year of the Prophet Muḥammad's prophethood. Containing 55 *āyāt*, it takes its title from the first *āyah*: 'The hour of Doom is drawing nearer, and the moon is cleft in two.'

Several prophets having had their warnings rejected by the people, the *sūrah* asks, 'Will any take heed?'

Recounting the story of the Prophet Nūh عليه السلام, it also tells of how at Allah's command, the rain ceased, the floods abated 'and His will was done and the Ark came to rest upon Mount Jūdi' (11:44). (A 7,700 feet mountain on the eastern borders of Turkey to the south of Lake Van and about 25 miles north-east of the town of Jazīrat Ibn ʿUmar, capital of the modern Syrian district al-Jazīra.) Allah 'left it as a sign so that people of later generations may take heed' (54:15).

Out of the entire Qur'ān, this *sūrah* contains one of the most compelling statements, which occurs four times: 'We have made the Qur'ān easy to remember: but will any take heed?' (54:17, 22, 32, and 40).

55
AR-RAḤMĀN
The Merciful

The *sūrah* was revealed at Madīnah and contains 78 *āyāt*. It takes its title from the Divine Name: 'The Merciful,' and hence the entire *sūrah* speaks of the mercies and blessings of Allah. Throughout the *sūrah*, the words, 'O which of the Lord's blessings would you deny?' are repeated 31 times.

The *sūrah* begins by affirming that the Qur'ān was revealed by Allah to the Prophet Muḥammad ﷺ, and goes on to tell of the creation of humanity and the unique arrangement for our physical sustenance. The universe is so full of the wondrous signs of Allah's creative power, that no individual of any sense could ever desist from praising and giving thanks to the Creator. But, in the face of these signs, there are people who choose to live in ignorance. This world is made for trial, therefore, we have complete freedom to choose the way we want to live. But, even then, no human or jinn has the freedom to run away beyond the boundaries of the universe (55:33). This amply proves that man is completely in the hands of Allah.

The *sūrah* gives a vivid description of Paradise and its delights. It asserts that those who successfully come through Allah's trials in this world will be eligible to enter the great Paradise of 'two gardens' (55:46).

56

AL-WĀQIʿAH

That Which Must Come to Pass

The *sūrah* was revealed at Makkah and contains 96 *āyāt*. The title is taken from the reference to the Day of Resurrection (*al-Wāqiʿah*) in the first *āyah,* as being 'that which must come to pass.' After giving a powerful description of the Hereafter, the *sūrah* says that on that Day, mankind shall be divided into three groups: the people on the right, the people on the left and those to the fore. The righteous will be on the right, while the sinners will be on the left. The third group, comprising the foremost (*aṣ-ṣābiqūn*), will be 'brought nearer to their Lord' (56:11). Of this third group the Prophet Muḥammad said, 'They are those who accepted the Truth the moment it was presented to them; when they were asked for the rights due from them, they gave them, and they judged others as they judged themselves' (Ibn Kathīr, *Tafsīr,* 4/283). For those who accepted Islam in its first phase, it was a discovery, while for later generations, it was a matter of inheritance rather than discovery. Thus, on the subject of the foremost, the *sūrah* aptly says that there will be 'a whole multitude from the people of old, but only a few from the later generations' (56:13).

The *sūrah* goes on to mention various phenomena of nature such as the process of human reproduction;

the seed that we grow in the soil; the drinking water which comes down from clouds as rain and is distributed through various rivers and springs; the fire which we use as fuel. All these things show tremendous power and intricately detailed planning on the part of the Almighty. We must reflect on these signs of Allah and give abundant thanks for these blessings.

The *sūrah* concludes by reaffirming the certainty of the Hereafter, and urges believers to praise the name of the Lord, the Supreme One.

57

AL-ḤADĪD

Iron

The *sūrah* was revealed at Madīnah and contains 29 *āyāt*. The title of the *sūrah* is derived from the mention of iron in *āyah* 25 as a source of physical power, symbolizing the firm stand of believers when called to the cause of Islam. The *sūrah* begins with powerful eulogies of Allah: 'It is He that has sovereignty over the heavens and the earth. He ordains life and death, and has power over all things. He is the First and the Last, the Visible and the Unseen…' The *sūrah* goes on to urge believers to donate generously to the cause of Allah and says that on the Day of Judgement, believing men and women will walk along with their light shining before them. The hypocrites will beg for the light to guide them. But they will be asked to 'go back and seek some other light. A wall with a gate will be set before them. Inside there shall be mercy, and out, to the fore, the scourge of Hell' (57:13, 14). *Āyāt* 20 and 21 warn that 'the life of this world is but a sport and a pastime.' It is like a green plant which flourishes only after a fall of rain and then soon turns yellow. Therefore, we should strive for the pardon of our Lord, and for a Paradise as vast as the heavens and the earth. The *sūrah* comforts believers by pointing out that any misfortune that befalls them is directly governed by Allah. Giving a message of hope, it enjoins them neither to grieve for the good things they miss, nor to be overjoyed at what they gain (57:22-24). The scriptures and scales of justice have been brought down, it maintains, so that people may 'conduct themselves with fairness' (57:25).

After mentioning the role of the Prophets Nūḥ and Ibrāhīm as Allah's messengers, the *sūrah* concludes by promising believers that those who fear Him and put their trust in His messenger, will be granted a double share of Allah's mercy—His light and His forgiveness.

58

AL-MUJĀDILAH

She Who Pleaded

This *sūrah*, revealed at Madīnah, contains 22 *āyāt*. The title refers to a Madīnan woman, Khawlah bint Thaᶜlabah, who was divorced by her husband simply saying: 'Be to me as my mother's back' (*antī ᶜalayya ka ẓahr ummī*). Recourse to this old pagan custom, *ẓihār*, deprived her of all marital rights, and made it impossible for her to remarry. In this helpless condition, with no one to support her and her little children, she took her pleas to the Prophet Muḥammad ﷺ. This *sūrah* was thereupon revealed, to condemn and abolish this old Arab custom. This Quranic injunction points out in general terms, the wife's right to plead against cruel and unjustified, marital separation.

The *sūrah* then reminds mankind that on the Day of Judgement, Allah 'will inform them of their actions,' which He has recorded, 'although they have forgotten them' (58:6). The *sūrah* goes on to say that 'if three people converse in secret, He is their fourth, if five, He is their sixth, whether fewer or more, wherever they be, He is with them' (58:8).

After dealing with ethical teachings, alms-giving, hypocrisy, etc., the *sūrah* concludes by saying that the believers are God's confederates: 'Allah is well pleased with them, and they are well pleased with Allah' (58:22).

59

AL-ḤASHR

The Gathering

The *sūrah* was revealed at Madīnah and contains 24 *āyāt*. The greater part of this *sūrah* deals with the conflict between the Muslims and the Jewish tribe of Banū Nadīr. After the Prophet Muḥammad's ﷺ migration to Madīnah, the Banū Nadīr tribe signed a treaty with the Prophet by which they were to remain neutral in the hostilities with the pagan Quraysh. But, quite to the contrary, during the battle of Uḥud the tribe broke the pact and allied themselves with the Makkan Quraysh against the tiny Muslim community. On that occasion the Prophet proposed two options, either war or their departure from Madīnah. They opted for the latter course, provided they could come back to the city once every year to collect their produce. But, once again, they conspired with the hypocrites of Madīnah, who had falsely promised to come to their rescue when they were forced to vacate their houses. The hypocrites' promise did not, however, materialize and ultimately they were expelled from the city. Most of them went to Adhraʿāt in Syria along with a caravan, while others settled in Khaybar.

The *sūrah* then conjures up the very striking image of what would have happened if the Qur'ān had been sent down on a mountain: people 'would have seen it humble itself and break asunder for fear of Allah' (59:21). The Quranic announcement of the great reality that we are not free, but accountable to an all-powerful Being Who observes our every deed, is such momentous news as to shake a mountain. But in their utter ignorance and heedlessness, some do not tremble at this awesome truth. The *sūrah* concludes with the mention of a number of Divine Names.

60

AL-MUMTAḤANAH

The Examined One

The *sūrah* was revealed in Madīnah after the Treaty of Ḥudaybiyyah and contains 13 *āyāt.* It deals mainly with relations between Muslims and non-Muslims, giving an injunction against entering into friendly relations with the enemies of Islam, such as the pagan Makkans, who not only expelled the Prophet and his followers from Makkah but waged incessant war against them. As regards relations with non-believers who are not actively hostile to Islam, the *sūrah* ordains kindness and friendliness towards them (60:8-9), regarding them as potential future Muslims:

Referring to certain problems arising after the treaty of Ḥudaybiyyah, the *sūrah* enjoins the Prophet Muḥammad ﷺ to test the women-folk migrating to Madīnah and not to send them back to the non-believers if they were found to be sincere in their faith. This is the circumstance that gives the *sūrah* its title.

61

AṢ-ṢAFF

The Ranks

The *sūrah* was revealed at Madīnah and contains 14 *āyāt*. It sums up the importance of unity, and urges the believers to be true to their word, as 'it is the most loathsome thing in Allah's sight that you should say one thing and do another' (61:3). Mentioning the Prophets ʿĪsā (Jesus) and Mūsā (Moses), the *sūrah* records the prophecy made by the Prophet ʿĪsā عليه السلام about the advent of the Prophet Muḥammad ﷺ: 'A prophet that shall come after me, whose name shall be Aḥmad' (61:6). Believers are also urged to have faith in Allah and His messenger, and to be ready to lay down their wealth and their lives for Allah's cause, which would stand them in good stead, like a 'profitable merchandise' (61:10) in terms of their fate in the Hereafter.

62

AL-JUMUʿAH

The Congregation on Friday

This *sūrah* of 11 *āyāt* was revealed at Madīnah. It begins by declaring that whatever is in the heavens and the earth is constantly praising and glorifying Almighty Allah. It defines the mission of the Prophet Muḥammad ﷺ as being to purify people's hearts and souls by conveying to them the divine message, so that they may understand the natural scheme of things and act accordingly.

The *sūrah* then instructs believers to stop trading, and hurry to the obligatory Friday prayer at the appointed time and then to disperse freely afterwards to seek Allah's bounty. (The occasion for the revelation of this *sūrah* was the sudden exit from the mosque of a part of the congregation, half-way through the Prophet's Friday Sermon, in order to meet a long-awaited caravan from Syria.) In other words, a true believer should constantly remember Allah during his worldly pursuits, and when he is called upon to carry out a religious obligation, he must give it priority over worldly advantage. Though this principle directly concerns the Friday prayer, it is applicable to all other religious responsibilities.

63

AL-MUNĀFIQŪN

The Hypocrites

The *sūrah* was revealed at Madīnah and contains 11 *āyāt*. After the Prophet's migration to Madīnah, the migrants (Muhājirūn) were helped by the Anṣār, the Muslims of Madīnah. The hypocrites of the city did not like this and tried to dissuade the Anṣār from helping them, saying: 'Spend nothing on those who are with Allah's Messenger, so that they may disperse' (63:7). During a campaign the leader of the hypocrites, ʿAbdullah ibn Ubayy, even uttered these words: 'When we return to Madīnah, the honourable will surely drive out those contemptible ones.' Little did the hypocrites know that 'honour belonged to Allah and His Messenger, and to those who believe (in Allah)' (63:8). The *sūrah* concludes by urging us to give charity. When our death approaches, no one will be given any extra time then to do good works or give charity (63:10-11).

64

AT-TAGHĀBUN

Mutual Loss and Gain

This *sūrah* of 18 *āyat*, revealed at Madīnah, derives its title from *āyah* 9, which calls the Day of Judgement 'the Day of Mutual Loss and Gain.' Real loss is loss in the Hereafter, just as real gain is gain in the Hereafter. The *sūrah* recalls how, when a prophet is raised from amongst the people, or a prophetic call is conveyed, they merely reject it by asking, 'Shall mortals be our guides?' (64:6).

Pointing out that 'your wealth and children are only a temptation,' the *sūrah* says that for some people their spouses and children act as their enemies (64:14). In the words of a *ḥadīth*, the Prophet Muḥammad ﷺ said, 'People will be brought on the Day of Judgement and will be told that all their good actions have been eaten up by their spouses and children.' Hence the Qur'ān enjoins the believers not to be niggardly in spending in the cause of Allah: 'Give a generous loan to Allah, He will multiply it for you and will forgive you' (64:17).

65

AṬ-ṬALĀQ

Divorce

The *sūrah* was revealed at Madīnah and contains 12 *āyāt*. Its title is derived from *āyah* 1, which deals with divorce. The rest of the *sūrah* is also devoted to aspects and problems of divorce, and the importance of the waiting period (*ʿiddah*) for women in the process of divorce. *Āyāt* 6 and 7 remind the believers to behave honourably towards women who are undergoing a waiting period, admonishing them not to harass them or make their lives intolerable, but rather to spend on them from what Allah has given them. This *sūrah* elaborates on *āyāt* 228–233 of *sūrah* 2: *al-Baqarah*.

AT-TAḤRĪM

The Prohibition

The *sūrah* was revealed at Madīnah and contains 12 *āyāt*. The title is taken from *āyah* 1, which asks the Prophet Muḥammad ﷺ why he has forbidden himself something which is lawful in the sight of Allah (according to some Commentators it was honey). The first half of the *sūrah* deals with certain aspects of the personal and family life of the Prophet. The believers are then asked to 'turn to Allah in sincere repentance' (66:8), which should not be merely a repetition of certain words, but the expression of the firm determination of the believer never to repeat any lapse which may earn Allah's anger.

The *sūrah* concludes by mentioning particular disbelieving and believing women—the wives of the Prophets Nūḥ and Lūṭ on the one hand, and the wife of Firᶜawn and Maryam on the other. The example of the first two women implies that even being in close relation to prophets will not save a sinner from the fire of Hell. On the other hand, if one lives righteously, no matter how unfavourable the circumstances may be, one earns Allah's pleasure, as in the case of the believing wife of Firᶜawn when she prayed: 'My Lord, build me a house in Paradise, in Your presence, and deliver me from Firᶜawn and his misdeeds' (66:11).

67

AL-MULK

Sovereignty

This *sūrah* of 30 *āyāt* was revealed at Makkah. After praising the Almighty, the *sūrah* declares that Allah has 'created death and life so that He might put you to a test to show which one of you is best in conduct' (67:2). While calling attention to the flawless creations of the Almighty, the *sūrah* challenges anyone to find a single flaw in the creation of the Merciful: 'Turn up your eyes: can you see any faults? Then look once more and yet again: your vision will fall back upon you, dazzled and defeated...' (67:3-4).

'When the sinners are cast into Hell, they shall hear it roaring and seething, as though it would burst with rage. They will be asked by the keepers of Hell whether or not anyone ever came to warn them. They will reply in the affirmative but will confess their sin in rejecting the warners' (67:7-9). 'Far from Allah's mercy are the heirs of Hell. But those that fear their Lord, without seeing Him, shall be forgiven and richly rewarded' (67:12).

The *sūrah* then says that whether you speak in secret or aloud, Allah knows your innermost thoughts: 'Shall He who has created all things not know them all?' (67:14). If people would only observe the birds above their heads, spreading their wings and closing them, they would surely see that 'none save the Merciful sustains them' (67:19). The *sūrah* goes on to urge us to give thanks to the Lord for bringing us into existence and for having given us ears, eyes and hearts (67:23).

The *sūrah* concludes with the assertion that 'if all the water that we have were to sink down into the earth, only Allah could give us running water in its place' (67:30).

68

AL-QALAM

The Pen

The *sūrah*, revealed at Makkah in 52 *āyāt,* begins by stressing the 'sublime character' of the Prophet Muḥammad ﷺ.

It tells of the owners of a fruit-laden orchard, who once decided to pluck its fruit the next morning without, however, saying, 'If Allah wills so.' A visitant from the Lord then descended upon their garden while they slept, utterly destroying its fruits. At daybreak they hurried there, selfishly whispering to one another, 'No poor man shall enter the orchard today.' But, once there they cried out, 'We are utterly ruined!' (68:17-27). This parable tells us that all our earnings come from the Almighty Allah. Those who regard these as a divine gift, will surely set aside a portion for the poor and needy.

On the Day of Judgement, those who rejected the call to prostrate themselves before their Lord, in this world will be unable to do so in the Hereafter (68:42-43).

The *sūrah* endes by mentioning the Prophet Yūnus (Jonah) عليه السلام and explaining that the Qur'ān is an admonition to mankind.

69

AL-ḤĀQQAH

The Impending Reality

The *sūrah* was revealed at Makkah about four years before the *hijrah* of the Prophet. It contains 52 *āyāt* and derives its name from *āyāt* 1–3, which refer to the Day of Judgement, as 'the impending reality.' Giving a powerful description of Judgement Day, the *sūrah* declares that 'on that Day you shall be utterly exposed, and not one secret of yours concealed' (69:18). On that Day those who are given their record book in their right hand will be among the dwellers of Paradise. But those who are given their book in their left hand will cry out: 'Would that my death had ended all! Nothing has my wealth availed me, and I am bereft of all my power' (69:27–28). The sinner would then be fettered with a chain seventy cubits in length and thrown into Hell, for 'he never believed in Allah, the Almighty, and he never urged the feeding of the poor' (69:33–34).

The *sūrah* concludes by saying that the Qur'ān is the revelation of the Lord of the Worlds, a reminder to the God-fearing and if the Prophet Muḥammad ﷺ had invented lies about Allah, he would have been seized and his heart's vein cut (69:45–51).

70
AL-MAʿĀRIJ
The Stairways

The *sūrah* was revealed at Makkah and contains 44 *āyāt*. Its title is drawn from *āyah* 3, which refers to Allah as 'the Lord of the Stairways.' This *sūrah* gives a vivid description of the Day of Judgement: 'On that Day the heavens shall become like molten brass, and the mountains like tufts of wool scattered in the wind. Friends will meet, but shall not speak to each other. To redeem himself (or herself) from the suffering of that Day, the sinner will gladly sacrifice his own children, his spouse, his brother, his kin, who always sheltered him, and everyone who lives on earth, if this then might deliver him. But all in vain (70:8-14).

The *sūrah* goes on to describe the true believers as those 'who are steadfast in prayer; give charity; who truly believe in the Day of Judgement and fear the punishment of their Lord; who are mindful of their chastity; and keep their trusts and promises and firmly stand to give witness' (70:23-34).

71

NŪḤ

Noah

The *sūrah* was revealed at Makkah and contains 28 *āyāt*. The entire *sūrah* is devoted to the call of the Prophet Nūḥ to his people. The essence of his call can be summed up in three words: *ʿibādah, taqwā* and *ṭāʿah,* that is, worship of Allah, piety, and obedience to the Prophet (71:3). This has been the call of every messenger of Allah and is also the true message of the Qur'ān. The Prophet Nūḥ continued calling his people to Allah day and night... loudly in public and secretly in private (71:5). But his people rejected him, thrusting their fingers in their ears and drawing their garments over their heads (71:7). The Prophet Nūḥ عليه السلام also reminded them to ponder the creations of the Almighty—the sky, the sun, the moon, the earth, the rivers, etc. (71:15-17). But his people continued to be proud and sinful. Ultimately the wicked were drowned in the great Flood.

The *sūrah* concludes with the prayer of the Prophet Nūḥ: 'My Lord, forgive me and my parents, and whosoever enters my house as a believer. Forgive all the faithful, men and women alike, and hasten the destruction of the wrongdoers!' (71:28).

72
AL–JINN
The Jinn

This *sūrah* was revealed at Makkah, about 2 years before the Prophet's *hijrah* to Madīnah. A company of jinn, after having listened to the Qur'ān, immediately believed in it and exclaimed: 'We have heard a wondrous Qur'ān giving guidance to the right path. We believe in it and shall henceforth serve none besides Our Lord' (72:1–2). According to the *sūrah*, there are both righteous and wicked among the jinn: 'Some of us have surrendered, others have deviated' (72:14). The jinn also state in this *sūrah* that they made their way 'to high heaven, and found it filled with mighty wardens (angels) and fiery comets. We sat there on seats to hear; but eavesdroppers find flaming darts in wait for them' (72:8–9).

The *sūrah* goes on to describe the prophetic mission—which is now the responsibility of Muslims—to make known the message of Allah (72:23).

73

AL-MUZZAMMIL

The Mantled One

The revelation of this *sūrah* belongs to the earliest Makkan period, and is regarded by commentators as being the third or fourth in order of revelation. It contains 20 *āyāt*.

The main theme of the *sūrah* is to urge believers to 'keep vigil all night, save for a few hours; half the night, or even less: or a little more' (73:2-3). The Prophet and his Companions were often up at night, rejecting sleep and giving themselves up to prayer and praise and the reading of the Qur'ān. Although religious observances are made obligatory, keeping in mind the abilities of ordinary people, there are acts which are desired 'beyond that which is incumbent on you.' The regularity with which the faithful perform such additional rites will determine their rewards in the Hereafter.

The *sūrah* reminds the believers to recite the Qur'ān calmly, distinctly and without any haste: 'Recite the Qur'ān with measured tone (*rattil'l-Qur'āna tarlīlan*).' This starts a two-way process between the Qur'ān and its reader. For readers, the Qur'ān becomes a divine address to which they respond as they read it *āyah* by *āyah*, word by word.

The 'words of surpassing gravity (*qawlan thaqīlan*)'

in *āyah* 5 refer to the order in the next *sūrah* (74): 'Arise and warn.' Warning people of the Hereafter is certainly the most difficult task, as the *dāʿī* (the caller), who takes up the call of Truth, becomes like a stranger among his or her own people, and sometimes has to endure the insufferable in order to maintain favourable relations between themselves and the *madʿū* (those non-Muslims to whom Islamic teaching is directed).

74
AL-MUDDATHTHIR
The Cloaked One

The *sūrah* was revealed at Makkah after the very first revelation of the Qur'ān. It contains 56 *āyāt* and the title is derived from *āyah* 1, which addresses the Prophet thus: 'You that are wrapped up in your cloak...' Though one of the earliest revelations, the *sūrah* outlines all the fundamental concepts of the Qur'ān, and focusses on the great responsibility of the Prophet and through him of all his followers to warn people about the Hereafter. The Prophet is asked in *āyāt* 1-5 to 'arise and give warning. Magnify your Lord, purify your garments, and shun uncleanness.'

The *sūrah* goes on to say that human pride is the root cause of our failure to recognize the Truth, and that 'each soul is the hostage of its own deeds' (74:38). Towards the end, the *sūrah* records a conversation between the denizens respectively of Paradise and Hell: 'What has brought you into Hell?' They replied: 'We never prayed, nor did we ever feed the hungry. We engaged in vain disputes and denied the Day of Reckoning, till the inevitable end overtook us' (74:41-47).

75

AL-QIYĀMAH

Resurrection

The *sūrah* was revealed at Makkah and contains 40 *āyāt*. Its title is derived from *āyah* 1 which begins, 'I swear by the Day of Resurrection...' The *sūrah* is a very strong reminder of the Day 'when the eyesight shall be dazed and the moon shall be darkened, and the sun and the moon shall be brought together—on that Day man will ask: "Whither shall I flee?" But there shall be no refuge. For on that Day to your Lord all shall return. On that Day humanity shall be told of all their deeds, from first to last. Indeed, man shall bear witness against himself, plead as he may with his excuses (75:8-15).

The *sūrah* chiefly draws attention to our own human nature—*nafs lawwāmah*—which distinguishes between good and evil. Thus we, by our very nature (*fiṭrah*), desire that evil-doers be punished and the righteous be rewarded. The very fact that we are of such a nature is a clear proof of the Hereafter.

The *sūrah* also commands the Prophet Muḥammad ﷺ not to be hasty in receiving the revelation of Allah, but rather to 'follow its words attentively' (75:18), as it is Allah Himself who will explain its meaning.

The *sūrah* concludes by condemning the idea that we have been left without a purpose. It stresses the seriousness of life and our responsibility for our actions. Thus the *sūrah* deplores man's heedlessness of the Day of Resurrection, and asserts that the Creator who originally created us from nothingness has indeed the power to 'raise the dead to life.'

76
AL-INSĀN
Man

The *sūrah* contains 31 *āyāt* and was revealed at Makkah. Some Commentators believe it belongs to the Madinan period. This *sūrah* is often called *ad-Dahr,* meaning 'Time.' Both the titles are derived from *āya* 1, which refers to the creation of man from nothingness: 'Has there not been over Man a time when he was nothing, when he was a thing unremembered?' The *sūrah* then explains the creation of humanity from 'sperm mixed (with ovum)'. This Quranic statement made so early as the 7th century is quite extraordinary: it proves the divine origin of the scripture by revealing a fact which came to be known only in the 20th century.

The main theme of the *sūrah* is the contrast between those who choose good and those who choose evil. It gives the example of the believers who do good deeds to win Allah's pleasure: 'They fulfill their vows and fear a Day whose terrors are far-spread; they feed the poor man, the orphan, and the captive, saying: "We feed you for Allah's sake only; we seek of you neither recompense nor thanks; for we fear from our Lord a day of anguish and woe"' (76:8-10).

The *sūrah* asks believers to 'remember the Name of your Lord at dawn and in the evening; bow down before Him and magnify Him at night: praise Him through the long night' (76:25,26). But many people are so ungrateful to their Lord that they 'love the hasty world, and leave behind them a grief-laden day' (76:27).

77

AL-MURSALĀT

Those Sent Forth

The *sūrah* was revealed at Makkah and contains 50 *āyāt*. The title is taken from the first *āya*, which refers to different kinds of winds sent forth by the Almighty. The constant refrain of the *sūrah* is 'Oh, woe on that day to the deniers,' an admonition which occurs ten times in its fifty *āyāt*. The *sūrah* presents a powerful description of the Day of Judgement, 'when the stars shall be blotted out, when the sky is rent asunder and the mountains crumble into dust' (77:18-10). On that Day the disbelievers will be asked to depart towards a 'triple-massing shadow, which will give neither shade nor shelter from the blazing flames' (77:30-31). The righteous, on the other hand, 'shall dwell amidst cool shades and fountains, and feed on such fruits as they desire' (77:41-42). The disbelievers, who did not bow to the Lord in this world, will on that Day be forbidden to kneel down to Him (77:48). The *sūrah* concludes by asking, when such clear guidance has already been offered to them: 'In what revelation, after this, will they believe?' (77:50).

78

AN-NABĀ'

The Tidings

The *sūrah* was revealed at Makkah and contains 40 *āyāt.* It is notable for its forceful descriptive style combined with its strong, rhythmic qualities. The *sūrah* begins by answering those who doubt whether there is life after death, urging them to ponder over the innumerable signs scattered throughout the universe, which are full of purpose and meaning, for example, the vast earth like a carpet, to which the mountains are pegs (78:6-7); the creation of beings in pairs (78:8), with work and rest succeeding each other in consonance with day and night (78:9-11); the splendid light of the sun, and the clouds and rain giving abundant harvests (78:13-16). All this will show that the universe is moving towards a purposeful future. Hence the *sūrah* warns: 'Surely the Day of Judgement is an appointed time, the day the Trumpet is blown. You shall come in multitudes. The gates of heaven shall swing open, and the mountains shall pass away and become like vapour. Behold, Hell lies in ambush' (78:17-21). The *sūrah* goes on to describe the life hereafter, where the wicked will drink foul things in Hell, while the righteous will enjoy the physical delights of Paradise. On that Day there will be no intercession, not even by angels, and the sinners will wish they were dust.

79

AN-NĀZIʿĀT

The Snatchers

The *sūrah* was revealed at Makkah and contains 46 *āyāt*. The title is derived from *āyah* 1, which refers to the winds that 'snatch away men's souls.' It depicts the Day of Resurrection, when a 'violent convulsion will take place, which will fill hearts with terror, and all eyes shall stare with awe.' People will wonder whether after death, they will be restored to life. 'But it shall be only a single quake, and behold, they are awakened.'

The *sūrah* goes on to tell of the confrontation between the Prophet Mūsā ﷺ and Firʿawn. When the latter denied Allah's 'mightiest sign, and said, "I am your Lord Most High," Allah smote him with the scourge of the Hereafter and of this life,' and he perished along with his followers.

Of those who do not believe in the Day of Resurrection, the *sūrah* asks, 'Are you more diffficult to create than the heaven which He has built?' (79:27). In other words, the Almighty, having created such a vast cosmos, certainly does have the power to raise the dead. Hence 'the transgressor, and the one who preferred the life of this world, will find his (or her) home in Hell.' While 'the one that feared to stand before his Lord and curbed his (or her) soul's desire shall have his (or her) home in Paradise' (79:37-41).

80

ʿABASA

He Frowned

An early Makkan *sūrah* of 42 *āyāt*, it takes its title from *āyah* 1, which relates how the Prophet Muḥammad ﷺ spoke roughly to a blind man, ʿAbdullāh ibn Umm Maktūm, who interrupted his explanation of the Qur'ān to certain chiefs of the pagan Quraysh. Thereupon this admonitory *sūrah* was revealed. The Prophet regretting his reaction, treated Ibn Umm Maktūm ever after with great respect, finally making him governor of Madīnah.

The *sūrah* describes the Qur'ān as a 'reminder... set down on honoured pages, purified and exalted, by the hands of noble and pious scribes.' It reminds people how ungrateful they are, though Allah has so miraculously created them from a drop of sperm and eased the way for them.' If we just reflect on our daily lives, we would be amazed to see 'how Allah has created our food, and how He pours down the rains abundantly, and cleaves the earth asunder; how He brings forth the corn, vegetables and fruits?' (80:17-32).

The *sūrah* concludes by depicting the Last Day: 'When the blast shall sound on that day, each man shall flee from his brother, and from his mother and father and his spouse and his children; for each of them will on that Day have enough sorrow of his own.'

81

AT-TAKWĪR

Shrouding in Darkness

Its revelation belongs to a very early Makkan period and contains 29 *āyāt.* Its title is taken from *āyah* 1, which begins with a powerfully rhythmic description of the Last Hour: 'When the sun ceases to shine; when the stars fall down and the mountains are blown away..., then each soul shall know what it has done. The *sūrah* also refers to the occasion when the Prophet Muḥammad ﷺ saw the angel Jibrīl in his original form, spreading his wings in the sky from east to west. The *sūrah* concludes by announcing that the Qur'ān is an admonition to mankind, to those who have the will to be upright (81:27-28).

82

AL-INFIṬĀR

The Cleaving Asunder

The *sūrah* was revealed at Makkah and contains 22 *āyāt*. It begins by depicting in very powerful words the approach of the Last Day: 'When the sky is cleft asunder; when the stars are scattered and the oceans burst beyond their bounds, when the graves are hurled about, each soul shall know what it has sent forth and what held back.'

Touching on our ingratitude to our Lord, the *sūrah* asks: 'What evil has enticed you from your generous Lord, who created you, gave you an upright form, and proportioned you? In whatever shape He willed, He could have moulded you.'

The *sūrah* also informs us that we are being watched by 'noble recorders who know what you do.' Knowing that some deny the Last Judgement, the *sūrah* concludes by exhorting us twice: 'Would that you knew what the Day of Judgement is!' It then informs us that it is the day when every soul will stand alone and the Lord will reign Supreme.

83

AL-MUṬAFFIFĪN

Those Who Give Short Measure

The *sūrah* was revealed at Makkah and contains 27 *āyāt*. It strongly condemns those who give short measure in their daily dealings, thereby cheating others. In other words, the truly sublime human character is one who is always ready to give equal rights to others. The *sūrah* mentions the names of two registers: *sijjīn*, which contains a record of all wrongdoers (83:7), and *ʿillīyūn*, which contains a record of the righteous (83:18). On account of their denial of the Hereafter, the sinners will not be allowed to see their Lord on the Day of Judgement (83:14). The *sūrah* goes on to describe the delights of Paradise. One such would be a pure sealed wine, tempered with the waters of the spring called Tasnīm and with a fragrance of musk. 'For this let all people compete' (83:25-27).

84

AL-INSHIQĀQ

The Splitting Apart

The *sūrah* was revealed at Makkah and contains 25 *āyāt*. The theme of the *sūrah* is the Last Day 'when the sky is rent apart, obeying her Lord in true submission; when the earth expands and casts out all that is within her and becomes empty, obeying her Lord in true submission.'

Describing the human condition as 'painful toiling towards the Lord,' the *sūrah* informs us that ultimately we will have to meet our Lord. On that Day, 'he that is given his book in his right hand shall have a lenient reckoning, and shall return rejoicing to his people. But he that is given his book behind his back shall call down destruction on himself and burn in the fire of Hell, for he lived without a care among his people and thought he would never return to Allah.' The *sūrah* ends in wonder at those who do not kneel down in prayer when the Qur'ān is read to them.

85

AL-BURŪJ

The Constellations

The *sūrah* was revealed at Makkah and contains 22 *āyāt*. The *sūrah* derives its name from *āyah* 1, which is an invocation: 'By the heaven with its constellations.' The first part of the *sūrah* refers to *Aṣḥāb al-Ukhdūd* (the makers of the fire-pits), who persecuted the believers.

The *sūrah* then goes on to describe the eternal power of Allah: 'Surely your Lord's grip is exceedingly strong! Surely it is He who originates, and brings again, and He is the All-forgiving, the All-loving, Lord of the throne, the All-glorious, the Executor of His own will.'

86

AṬ-ṬĀRIQ

The Star

The *sūrah* was revealed at Makkah and contains 17 *āyāt*. The title is taken from the invocation in *āyah* 1: 'By the heaven and the night star!' The *sūrah* goes on to remind us that 'for every soul there is a guardian watching it.'

It then asks humanity 'to reflect from what he (or she) is created,' and explains that 'he is created from an ejaculated fluid that issues from between the loins and the ribs.' The Almighty, who has created us from nothingness 'surely has the power to bring us back to life, on that Day when all secrets will be laid bare and we will have neither strength nor helper!' Of the Qur'ān, the *sūrah* goes on to declare: 'This is indeed a discerning utterance, and is no idle tale' (86:13-14). It concludes by counselling the believers to be patient with the deniers of the Truth: 'Let them have their will for a little while.'

87

AL-AᶜLĀ

The Most High

The *sūrah* was revealed at Makkah and contains 19 *āyāt*. It takes its name from *āyah* 1, which asks believers to 'praise the Name of your Lord, the Most High.' It goes on to narrate the blessing of Allah, 'who has created all things and proportioned them; who has ordained their destinies and guided them; who brings forth the green pasture, then turns it to withered grass.'

Addressing the Prophet Muḥammad ﷺ, Allah says: 'We will teach you (Our revelations), so that you shall forget none of them except as Allah pleases.'

The *sūrah* enjoins him to proclaim the divine Message to all: 'Give warning, if warning will avail. He that fears Allah will heed it.' The *sūrah* comes to an end by saying 'Happy shall be the one who purifies himself (or herself), who remembers the name of the Lord and prays.' Yet people prefer this worldly life, 'although the life to come is better and more lasting.'

88

AL-GHĀSHIYAH

The Calamity

This *sūrah*, revealed at Makkah contains 26 *āyāt*, *al-Ghāshiyah* being one of the names of the Day of Resurrection. One of many powerful passages of the Qur'ān, it graphically captures the essence of the Day of Judgement: 'On that day there shall be downcast faces, of people broken and worn out, burnt by a scorching fire, drinking from a seething fountain. Their only food shall be bitter thorns...' (88:2-6).

Depicting the scene in Paradise, the *sūrah* goes on to says: 'On that day there shall be radiant faces, of people well-pleased with their labours, in a lofty garden. There they shall hear no idle talk. A gushing fountain shall be there, and raised soft couches with goblets placed before them; silken cushions ranged in order and carpets richly spread' (88:8-16).

The *sūrah* then reminds us of Allah's numerous blessings, which should lead us in awe to Him. Those who derive food for thought from the system of the world, who give sincere thanks to the Almighty for his blessings, and live assiduously in the way of Allah, will deserve Paradise as their eternal abode, while those who deliberately choose ignorance and evil will deserve to be denied Allah's blessings forever.

89

AL-FAJR

The Dawn

Of the early Makkan period, this *sūrah* of 30 *āyāt* derives its title from the oath expressed in *āyah* 1. Recalling the punishments Allah inflicted on the people of ʿĀd and Thamūd and on Firʿawn, it urges us to be kind to orphans and the needy, and to respect 'the inheritance of the weak' (89:17-19). It also warns us that when we see the terrors which precede the Day of Judgement, when 'Hell is brought near,' it will be too late to 'remember our deeds' (89:23).

As the *sūrah* explains, prosperity and poverty are both meant to try us in this world. Those who have an excessive desire for the material things of this life, who take a pride in being rich and become depressed when any calamity befalls them, will fail the divine test. On the other hand, those whose prosperity induces in them the virtues of humility and gratitude, will, when overtaken by distress, fall prostrate before their Lord, unashamed of how powerless they are. Termed a *nafs muṭma'innah*—a soul at peace, or a serene soul (89:27), he or she will be asked by the Almighty to enter Paradise:

> O soul at peace, return to your Lord, well-pleased, well-pleasing. Join My servants and enter My Paradise.
> (89:28-30)

90

AL-BALAD

The City

This *sūrah* was revealed at Makkah and contains 20 *āyāt*. The title is derived from a reference to Makkah, the city where the Prophet Muḥammad ﷺ was born and brought up. It underlines the face that human beings seem born to a life of toil and hardship. The fact that they can never set themselves free from hardships is a clear proof that they are subordinate to a far superior Being. *Āyat* 8-10 refer to our power of sight, hearing and speech. This too points towards a higher Being Who is observing and listening to us. Thus if we could recognise ourselves, we would recognize our Creator (cf. 41:53).

Allah has shown us two paths. One is the path of charity and kindness towards our fellow beings, especially towards orphans and the needy, the freeing of slaves from bondage and the feeding of the poor (90:10-16). Individuals who follow this path will, according to the *sūrah*, enjoin upon each other patience, kindness and compassion. On the Day of Judgement, they will stand on the right hand and will dwell in Paradise. Those who follow the other path by rejecting the divine revelation will, on the Day of Judgement, stand on the left hand side and will be condemned to Hell-fire (90:17-20).

91

ASH-SHAMS

The Sun

The *sūrah* was revealed at Makkah and contains 15 *āyāt*. It sums up the three-fold system formed by the Almighty for the guidance of mankind. First, the vast universe as a physical manifestation of the divine will. Second, the deep and instinctive knowledge of both piety and immorality invested in every human soul. Third, the coming of the prophets to make the difference between truth and falsehood clear. Given this divine scheme of things, if any stray from the right path, they become sinners in the sight of Allah.

The concluding story of the Prophet Ṣāliḥ عليه السلام shows that respect is due to righteous people, however helpless and weak they might be.

92

AL-LAYL

The Night

This *sūrah* was revealed at Makkah and contains 21 *āyāt*. The title is derived from the invocation in *āyah* 1: 'By the night as it veils in darkness'. The main theme of the *sūrah* is charity and the fear of God: 'For the one that gives in charity and guards against evil and believes in goodness, We shall smooth the path of salvation' (92:5-7).

On the contrary, the *sūrah* warns anyone 'who is a miser and indifferent and disbelieves in goodness' of ultimate hardship. The *sūrah* concludes by giving glad tidings to one 'who spends his wealth (on others) to purify himself, and who owes no favour to anyone, seeking only to win the pleasure of his Lord, the Most High.'

93

AḌ-ḌUḤĀ

The Morning Light

This *sūrah* was revealed at Makkah and contains 11 *āyāt,* the title being derived from *āyah* 1. When a period of some time had elapsed during which the Prophet received no further revelations after his first one, his opponents in Makkah began to taunt him, saying, 'Your God has forsaken and scorned you.' The Prophet thereupon received a message of hope and consolation: 'Your Lord has not forsaken you, nor is He displeased.' Reminding the Prophet of Allah's succour when he was orphaned, the *sūrah* urges that other orphans should not be oppressed.

94
ASH-SHARḤ
Solace

Revealed at Makkah in 8 *āyāt*, this *sūrah* directly addresses the Prophet Muḥammad ﷺ, and through him, every true believer of the Qur'ān. It reminds the Prophet of his great burden of anxiety about how to raise a fallen people from their ignorance and superstitions. It was Divine revelation that ultimately guided his steps towards achieving this goal (94:1–3). When Allah chose him as His last Prophet. *Āyah* 4 is a prophecy, made at a time when the Prophet was alone and unknown, of the glorious eminence to which he was to be raised. When the Prophet began to convey Allah's message, he met with stiff resistance from his own people, a factor which was the unwitting cause of Islam's spread throughout Arabia.

Thus the *sūrah* unfolds for every individual the divine principle, that this world is created by Allah in such a way that problems and opportunities exist here side by side. Only those who accept this and who steadfastly and patiently seek opportunities to improve their lot will be rewarded for their pains. Hence the *sūrah* declares: 'Surely with every hardship comes ease, with every hardship comes ease' (94:5–6).

95

AT-TĪN

The Fig

One of the very early *sūrahs,* it was revealed at Makkah and contains 8 *āyāt.* The title is taken from the invocation in *āyah* 1. The *sūrah* begins with the invocation of four things, the Fig, the Olive, Mount Sinai and the Secure City. According to the Commentators, the Fig and Olive are two mountains located near Jerusalem, which mean that the *āyah* refers to the area associated with the Prophet ʿĪsā عليه السلام. Mount Sinai is where the Prophet Mūsā was blessed with divine revelation. The Secure City is Makkah, where the Prophet Muḥammad ﷺ received the prophethood.

Allah has 'created humanity in a most noble image' (95:4) and endowed us with all the qualities, so that we may use them to recognise the Truth which Allah has sent through his prophets, and 'do good works, for theirs shall be a boundless recompense.' We were born in pure form, pure of every sin, but due to our wrongdoings we descend to 'the lowest of the low' (95:5).

96

AL-ʿALAQ

The Germ-Cell

This *sūrah* was revealed at Makkah and contains 19 *āyāt*, the first 5 *āyāt* of which were the very beginning of the revelation of the Qur'ān. The title of the *sūrah* is derived from *āyah* 2, which refers to human creation from a germ-cell. The *sūrah* emphasises the significance of acquiring knowledge, but warns that people transgress in thinking themselves their own masters; 'for to your Lord all things return' (96:6-8).

Āyāt 9-14 refer to the persecution of the Prophet Muḥammad ﷺ at the hands of Abū Jahl, who even tried to prevent the Prophet and his Companions from praying before the Kaʿbah. Such individuals who deny the Truth and obstruct its path will surely be cast into the Fire of Hell.

The *sūrah* concludes by asking us to bow down to the Almighty in worship: 'Prostrate yourself and come close (to Him).'

97

AL-QADR

The Night of Power

The *sūrah* was revealed at Makkah and contains 5 *āyāt.* The title is taken from the reference to the Night of Power (*laylat al-qadr*) in the first *āyah.* The Qur'ān began to be revealed on this night, which according to several Traditions of the Prophet, may be one of the last ten nights, probably the 27th, of the month of Ramaḍān. The Night is 'better than a thousand months.' On this Night 'the angels and the Spirit (Jibrīl) come down by their Lord's leave' (97:3-4). Due to the presence of an overwhelming number of angels on this night, a special kind of spiritual atmosphere prevails. Thus the seekers of spiritual gain on this night can find an extremely high level of spiritual nourishment.

98

AL-BAYYINAH

The Clear Proof

This *sūrah* was revealed at Madīnah and contains 8 *āyāt*. The title is derived from *āya* 1, which refers to the demand of disbelievers and polytheists for a 'clear proof,' such as a miracle or an angel descending to them from heaven. The *sūrah* ends with a reference to the Companions of the Prophet Muḥammad ﷺ: 'Well pleased is Allah with them, and they are well pleased with Him.'

99

AZ-ZALZALAH

The Earthquake

This *sūrah* was revealed at Makkah and contains 8 *āyāt*. It takes its name from the first *āyah* which refers to the tremendous convulsion which will take place on the Day of Resurrection. On that Day 'when Earth is rocked in her last convulsion; when Earth shakes off her burdens, and people cry out: "What may this mean?"—on that Day she will proclaim her tidings, for your Lord will have inspired her' (99:2-5).

Every single action or utterance of an individual is recorded in this world by the angels of Allah, as if the world were a vast 'recording studio' of the Almighty. And on the Day of Judgement when 'mankind will come in broken bands,' their acts, actions, utterances, even thoughts will be played back on the divine screen. So 'whoever does an atom's weight of good shall see it, and whoever does an atom's weight of evil shall see it too' (99:7-8).

100

AL-ʿĀDIYĀT

The War Horses

This *sūrah* was revealed at Makkah, and contains 11 *āyāt*. The title is derived from the first *āyah*. *Āyāt* 6–11 are a powerful reminder of our ignorance and pettiness in this world, and of our resurrection on the Day of Judgement: We are most ungrateful towards our Sustainer and passionate in our love for wealth. But are we not aware that when the dead are thrown out from their graves and their 'hidden thoughts are laid open, their Lord will on that Day have full knowledge of them all?'

101

AL-QĀRIʿAH

The Crushing Catastrophe

The *sūrah* was revealed at Makkah and contains 11 *āyāt*. It takes its name from the first *āyah* which refers to the sudden approach of the Last Hour. Giving a vivid description of the end of this world, the *sūrah* states that 'on that Day men shall become like scattered moths and the mountains like tufts of carded wool' (101:4-5). The *sūrah* concludes by saying that on the Last Day, man's virtues and vices will be weighed against each other: 'Then he whose scales are heavy shall dwell in bliss; but he whose scales are light, the Abyss shall be his home' (101:6-9).

102

AT-TAKĀTHUR

Greed for More and More

It was revealed at Makkah and contains 8 *āyāt.* The *sūrah* is a powerful admonition of man's unbounded greed for worldly gain, which preoccupies his heart and soul until he reaches the grave. But certainly he will know the Truth on the Day of Judgement, when he will see Hell with his very own eyes. On that Day, he will be questioned about the blessings and bounties which were granted to him.

During the time of severe persecution of the Makkan Quraysh, the Prophet ﷺ and his Companions had to pass long days in starvation. On one such day, the Prophet was passing through a street of Makkah along with Abū Bakr. A Companion who saw the Prophet, sensing that he had not eaten food for days, rushed to his house to fetch some fresh dates. The Prophet ate them with pleasure and exclaimed: 'This is the blessing (*naᶜīm*) which we shall be questioned about.'

103

AL-ʿAṢR

The Time

It was revealed at Makkah and contains only 3 *āyāt*. The *sūrah* insists that people will be lost unless they have faith and do good works, and 'exhort each other to justice and to fortitude.'

Imām Rāzī writes in his *Tafsīr Kabīr* that he understood the meaning of *sūrah al-ʿAṣr* from an ice-seller, who was urging people to buy his ice by saying, 'Be kind to the man whose wealth is being melted away, Be kind...' As he heard this voice, he said to himself: 'As the ice is melting away, so is the age of man passing quickly. If one lets this chance slip away, or sinfully misuses it, then one is the loser.'

104
AL-HUMAZAH
The Slanderer

The *sūrah* was revealed at Makkah and contains 8 *āyāt*. The title is derived from *āyah* 1, which condemns those who maliciously try to reveal faults in others. The *sūrah* excoriates 'every backbiting slanderer who amasses wealth,' thinking their wealth will make them live forever. Then it goes on to say, 'By no means! He (or she) shall be flung to the Destroying Flame,' 'Allah's own kindled fire, which will rise up to people's hearts. It will close upon them from every side, in towering columns.'

105

AL-FĪL

The Elephant

This *sūrah* of 5 *āyāt* was revealed at Makkah and derives its title from the reference to the elephants of the army of Abraha, the Ethopian Christian King, who ruled Yemen in the 6th century A.D. Intending to destroy the Kaᶜbah, he set out for Makkah, placing himself at the head of an army of sixty thousand men accompanied by a dozen elephants. However, when Abrahah was within a short distance of Makkah, his elephants refused to go any further. A flock of birds—*abābīl*—flew over them, showering them with small stones (*sijjīl*). This caused an epidemic of sores and pustules among the soldiers, and they fled. Many of them, including Abrahah himself, died on the way back: 'Have you not seen how the Lord dealt with the Army of the Elephants? Did He not make their treacherous plan go awry? And loose upon them flocks of birds, which pelted them with stones of baked clay, so that they became like the withered stalks of plants which cattle have devoured?' (105:1-6)

This incident occured in A.D. 570, the year of the Prophet Muḥammad's birth. This was a sign that whoever set himself against the Prophet or his mission would be destroyed like the army of the elephants.

106

QURAYSH

Revealed at Makkah, the *sūrah* contains 4 *āyāt*. Being the custodians of the Kaʿbah, the Quraysh tribe were held in high esteem throughout Arabia. This gave them a number of privileges. One such privilege was that in an age of general insecurity, their trade caravans were not attacked, resulting in great prosperity for the tribe. The *sūrah* reminds them that while deriving worldly benefit from being the custodians of the Kaʿbah, they must not forget the other responsibilities attached to it. In other words, they were urged to worship Allah by responding to the call of Truth brought to them by the Prophet Muḥammad ﷺ. In general, every individual is reminded here to be thankful to the Lord and worship Him, Who alone has the power to provide sustenance and establish peace.

107

AL-MĀʿŪN

Neighbourly Assistance

The *sūrah* contains 7 *āyāt* and was revealed at Makkah. The title is derived from *āyah* 7, which refers to individuals who fail to offer the least neighbourly help or charity. The *sūrah* draws attention to the 'one who denies the Last Judgement and who turns away the orphans and does not urge the feeding of the poor.' Individuals whose hearts are empty of Faith, thinking they are not accountable to their Lord, will not extend even the slightest courtesy or kindness to their fellow human beings. They may put on a pretence of doing good deeds, but this will be of no real help to others. The *sūrah* also admonishes those who are 'heedless in their prayer.'

108

AL-KAWTHAR

Good in Abundance

This *sūrah* was revealed at Makkah and contains 3 *āyāt.* The title is taken from *āyah* 1, which states that Allah gave 'abundance' to the Prophet Muḥammad ﷺ. *Āyah* 2 urges the Prophet to pray to Allah and make sacrifices. The *sūrah* concludes by telling him that 'his enemies would indeed be cut off.'

At the time when the *sūrah* was revealed, the Prophet was facing stiff resistance from the Makkan Quraysh. This was on account of his message of Truth. Only a handful of people had responded his call. At that painful moment, the *sūrah* was a message of hope to the Prophet and to the new Muslims. In later days the exemplary success of the Prophet proved true the words of the Qur'ān. If the Muslims were to take up the true cause of Islam, following in the footsteps of the Prophet, the same promise would apply to them—abundant good in this life and the life to come. According to a *ḥadīth* of Bukhārī, Kawthar is the name of a pond, or spring, where the followers of the Prophet Muḥammad ﷺ were allowed to quench their thirst before entering Paradise.

109
AL-KĀFIRŪN
Those Who Reject Faith

The *sūrah* belongs to the late Makkan period and contains 6 *āyāt.* The *sūrah* begins by asking the Prophet Muḥammad ﷺ not to concern himself with trying to force non-believers into the faith, but simply to bear witness and to say to the unbelievers, 'I do not worship what you worship, nor do you worship what I worship.' These words were revealed to the Prophet to exempt him from obligation towards such individuals as rejected his call, even after his unremitting efforts to convey Allah's message over a long period of thirteen years.

'To you your religion, and to me my religion' is not an endorsement of the religions of others: it proclaims rather the firm stand taken on the faith while accepting the non-believer's intransigence. Thus it teaches us to practice tolerance with non-Muslims and tells us to treat them with respect.

110

AN-NAṢR

Succour

The *sūrah* belongs to the Madīnan period and is one of the last words of the Qur'ān revealed to the Prophet.

Allah's special succour always accompanies *da*ʿ*wah*. The Prophet Muḥammad's ﷺ untiring efforts in this task created such circumstances during his last days (A.H. 9-10) that people in their thousands began embracing Islam. Due to this a number of neighbouring countries entered the fold of Islam. But the victory of believers makes them humble and more conscious of their own failings, hence the *sūrah* reminds:

> When comes the succour of Allah, and victory,
> and you see people entering Allah's religion in
> their thousands, then extol the glory
> of your Lord, and seek His forgiveness,
> for He is ever an accepter of repentence.
>
> (110:1-3)

111

AL-MASAD

Fibre

The *sūrah* was revealed at Makkah and contains 5 *āyāt.* The title of the *sūrah* comes from *āyah* 5 which refers to a rope of fibre.

Once Abū Lahab, an uncle of the Prophet Muḥammad ﷺ, yet his most violent enemy, took up a stone to cast at him, whereupon the *sūrah* was revealed:

> Let the hands of Abū Lahab perish,
> and let himself perish!
> Nothing shall his wealth and his gain avail him.
> Burned shall he be at a fiery flame;
> And his wife, laden with faggots;
> Shall have on her neck a rope of palm-fibre.
>
> (111:1-5)

112

AL-IKHLĀṢ

Oneness

The *sūrah* was revealed at Makkah and contains only 4 *āyāt*. The Prophet Muḥammad ﷺ once described this *sūrah* as 'equivalent to one-third of the whole of the Qur'ān' (Bukhārī, Muslim).

The subject of the *sūrah* is monotheism, or the oneness of Allah. It reaffirms the concept of God, placing Him above and apart from the debasing superstitions which have persisted throughout the ages. God is not many, He is only one. Everyone needs Him, while He does not need anyone. He reigns over all things of the heavens and the earth. Unlike human beings, He has no son or father. He is Eternal, without beginning or end, and is thus a unique Being Who has no equal:

> Say: He is Allah, One,
> Allah, the Eternal,
> Who has not begotten,
> nor has He been begotten
> and there is nothing that
> would be compared with Him.
>
> (112: 1-4)

113

AL-FALAQ

Daybreak

The *sūrah* was revealed at Makkah and contains 5 *āyāt*. The title of the *sūrah* is derived from *āyah* 1, which asks people to seek refuge with 'the Lord of the Daybreak.'

Since the present world is a place of test and trial, both good and evil will always exist here. The only way not to be affected by evils such as envy, magic and sorcery, is by seeking refuge with Almighty Allah, who alone has the power to save us from them. Hence the *sūrah* counsels:

> Say: 'I take refuge with the Lord of the daybreak
> from the evil of what He has created
> from the evil of darkness when it gathers,
> from the evil of those who blow on knots,
> from the evil of an envier when he envies.'
> (113:1-5)

114
AN-NĀS
Humankind

The *sūrah* was revealed at Makkah and contains 6 *āyāt*. The title is derived from *āyah* 1, which counsels the believers to 'seek refuge with the Lord of humankind.' The *sūrah* is a prayer to the Almighty to grant refuge from the mischief of evil-doers, both human and occult, and especially from their evil temptations:

> Say: 'I take refuge with the Lord of humankind,
> the King of humankind, the God of humankind,
> from the evil of those who whisper,
> in human hearts;
> from jinn and humankind.'
>
> (114:1-6)

GLOSSARY

Āyah (pl. *āyāt*)	Verse of the Qur'ān.
Commentator	Commentators on the Qur'ān. It usually mean the early Commentators such as Ṭabarī, Ibn Kathīr etc.
Companion	*Ṣaḥābah*, or the Companions of the Prophet Muḥammad ﷺ.
Dāʿī	One who gives the call to Islam.
Daʿwah	The call to Islam.
Ḥadīth (pl. *aḥādīth*)	A tradition or saying of the Prophet Muḥammad ﷺ.
Ḥadīth	Compilations of the Prophet Muḥammad's sayings.
Jihād	Lit., 'striving.' Any earnest striving for the cause of Allah, involving either personal effort or material resources.
Madʿū	One to whom the Islamic call is directed.
Ṣaḥābah (sing. *ṣaḥābī; ṣāḥib*)	Companion of the Prophet.
Ṣalāt	Prayers.
Ṣawm	Fasting.
Shariʿah	The moral and legal code of Islam based on the Qur'ān and the *sunnah* (see below) of the Prophet Muḥammad ﷺ.
Sunnah	The Teachings and practice of the Prophet Muḥammad ﷺ to be followed.
Sūrah (pl. *suwar*)	Chapter of the Qur'ān.
Ummah	The universal Muslim community.
ʿUmrah	Lesser pilgrimage.
Zakāt	Alms due.

Goodword English Publications

The Holy Quran: Text,Translation and Commentary (HB), Tr. Abdullah Yusuf Ali

The Holy Quran (PB), Tr. Abdullah Yusuf Ali

The Holy Quran (Laminated Board), Tr. Abdullah Yusuf Ali

The Holy Quran (HB), Tr. Abdullah Yusuf Ali

Holy Quran (Small Size), Tr. Abdullah Yusuf Ali

The Quran, Tr. T.B. Irving

The Koran, Tr. M.H. Shakir

The Glorious Quran, Tr. M.M. Pickthall

Allah is Known Through Reason, Harun Yahya

The Basic Concepts in the Quran, Harun Yahya

Crude Understanding of Disbelief, Harun Yahya

Darwinism Refuted, Harun Yahya

Death Resurrection Hell, Harun Yahya

Devoted to Allah, Harun Yahya

Eternity Has Already Begun, Harun Yahya

Ever Thought About the Truth?, Harun Yahya

The Mercy of Believers, Harun Yahya

The Miracle in the Ant, Harun Yahya

The Miracle in the Immune System, Harun Yahya

The Miracle of Man's Creation, Harun Yahya

The Miracle of Hormones, Harun Yahya

The Miracle in the Spider, Harun Yahya

The Miracle of Creation in DNA, Harun Yahya

The Miracle of Creation in Plants, Harun Yahya

The Moral Values of the Quran, Harun Yahya

The Nightmare of Disbelief, Harun Yahya

Perfected Faith, Harun Yahya

Bouquet of the Noble Hadith, Assad Nimer Busool

Forty Hadith, Assad Nimer Busool

Hijrah in Islam, Dr. Zafarul Islam Khan

Palestine Documents, Dr. Zafarul Islam Khan

At the Threshold of New Millennium, Dr. Zafarul Islam Khan

Islamic Sciences, Waqar Husaini

Islamic Thought..., Waqar Husaini

The Qur'an for Astronomy, Waqar Husaini

A Dictionary of Muslim Names, Prof. S.A. Rahman

Let's Speak Arabic, Prof. S.A. Rahman

Teach Yourself Arabic, Prof. S.A. Rahman

Islamic Medicine, Edward G. Browne

Literary History of Persia (Vol.1 & 2), Edward G. Browne

Literary History of Persia (Vol.3 & 4), Edward G. Browne

The Soul of the Quran, Saniyasnain Khan

Presenting the Quran, Saniyasnain Khan

The Wonderful Universe of Allah, Saniyasnain Khan

A-Z Ready Reference of the Quran (Based on the Translation by Abdullah Yusuf Ali), Mohammad Imran Erfani

The Alhambra, Washington Irving

The Encyclopaedic Index of the Quran, Dr. Syed Muhammad Osama

The Essentials of Islam, Al-Haj Saeed Bin Ahmed Al Lootah

Glossary of the Quran, Aurang Zeb Azmi

Introducing Arabic, Michael Mumisa

Arabic-English Dictionary, J.G. Hava

The Arabs in History, Prof. Bernard Lewis

A Basic Reader for the Holy Quran, Syed Mahmood Hasan

The Beauty of Makkah and Madinah, Mohamed Amin

A Brief Illustrated Guide to Understanding Islam, I.A. Ibrahim

The Concept of Society in Islam and Prayersin Islam, Dr. Syed Abdul Latif

Decisive Moments in the History of Islam, Muhammad Abdullah Enan

The Handy Concordance of the Quran, Aurang Zeb Azmi

Quick Grasp of Faith, Harun Yahya

Timelessness and the Reality of Fate, Harun Yahya

In Search of God, Maulana Wahiduddin Khan

Islam and Peace, Maulana Wahiduddin Khan

An Islamic Treasury of Virtues, Maulana Wahiduddin Khan

The Moral Vision, Maulana Wahiduddin Khan

Muhammad: A Prophet for All Humanity, Maulana Wahiduddin Khan

Principles of Islam, Maulana Wahiduddin Khan

Prophet Muhammad : A Simple Guide to His Life, Maulana Wahiduddin Khan

The Quran for All Humanity, Maulana Wahiduddin Khan

The Quran: An Abiding Wonder, Maulana Wahiduddin Khan

Religion and Science, Maulana Wahiduddin Khan

Simple Wisdom (HB), Maulana Wahiduddin Khan

Simple Wisdom (PB), Maulana Wahiduddin Khan

The True Jihad, Maulana Wahiduddin Khan

Tabligh Movement, Maulana Wahiduddin Khan

A Treasury of the Quran, Maulana Wahiduddin Khan

Woman Between Islam and Western Society, Maulana Wahiduddin Khan

Woman in Islamic Shari'ah, Maulana Wahiduddin Khan

The Ideology of Peace, Maulana Wahiduddin Khan

Indian Muslims, Maulana Wahiduddin Khan

Introducing Islam, Maulana Wahiduddin Khan

Islam: Creator of the Modern Age, Maulana Wahiduddin Khan

Islam: The Voice of Human Nature, Maulana Wahiduddin Khan

Islam Rediscovered, Maulana Wahiduddin Khan

Words of the Prophet Muhammad, Maulana Wahiduddin Khan

God Arises, Maulana Wahiduddin Khan

The Call of the Qur'an, Maulana Wahiduddin Khan

Building a Strong and Prosperous India and Role of Muslims, Maulana Wahiduddin Khan

Islam As It Is, Maulana Wahiduddin Khan

Sermons of the Prophet Muhammad, Assad Nimer Busool